Policarpio L. Mabborang Jr.
Juvylyn C. Amor

Estimating Earthquake Risk: The use of REDAS in the Philippines

AF141268

Policarpio L. Mabborang Jr.
Juvylyn C. Amor

Estimating Earthquake Risk: The use of REDAS in the Philippines

LAP LAMBERT Academic Publishing

Impressum / Imprint

Bibliografische Information der Deutschen Nationalbibliothek: Die Deutsche Nationalbibliothek verzeichnet diese Publikation in der Deutschen Nationalbibliografie; detaillierte bibliografische Daten sind im Internet über http://dnb.d-nb.de abrufbar.
Alle in diesem Buch genannten Marken und Produktnamen unterliegen warenzeichen-, marken- oder patentrechtlichem Schutz bzw. sind Warenzeichen oder eingetragene Warenzeichen der jeweiligen Inhaber. Die Wiedergabe von Marken, Produktnamen, Gebrauchsnamen, Handelsnamen, Warenbezeichnungen u.s.w. in diesem Werk berechtigt auch ohne besondere Kennzeichnung nicht zu der Annahme, dass solche Namen im Sinne der Warenzeichen- und Markenschutzgesetzgebung als frei zu betrachten wären und daher von jedermann benutzt werden dürften.

Bibliographic information published by the Deutsche Nationalbibliothek: The Deutsche Nationalbibliothek lists this publication in the Deutsche Nationalbibliografie; detailed bibliographic data are available in the Internet at http://dnb.d-nb.de.
Any brand names and product names mentioned in this book are subject to trademark, brand or patent protection and are trademarks or registered trademarks of their respective holders. The use of brand names, product names, common names, trade names, product descriptions etc. even without a particular marking in this work is in no way to be construed to mean that such names may be regarded as unrestricted in respect of trademark and brand protection legislation and could thus be used by anyone.

Coverbild / Cover image: www.ingimage.com

Verlag / Publisher:
LAP LAMBERT Academic Publishing
ist ein Imprint der / is a trademark of
OmniScriptum GmbH & Co. KG
Heinrich-Böcking-Str. 6-8, 66121 Saarbrücken, Deutschland / Germany
Email: info@lap-publishing.com

Herstellung: siehe letzte Seite /
Printed at: see last page
ISBN: 978-3-659-78061-5

Zugl. / Approved by: Tuguegarao City, Cagayan State University, 2014 Funded Research

Table of Contents

PREFACE

This book can be considered as one major output from the conduct of the Regional Disaster Science and Management S&T Capacity Development Project in Region 2 - Cagayan Province, Philippines. The project was funded by the Philippine Council for Industry, Engineering & Emerging Technology Research & Development (PCIEERD) of the Department of Science & Technology (DOST). Implementation of the project was made possible with the assistance extended by the team from the Philippine Institute of Volcanology and Seismology (PHIVOLCS). Scientific paper presentations were rendered along the same topic during the 10th Asian Seismological Commission General Assembly (ASC 2014) and during the 1st International Research and Education Conference for the Academe of Today which was sponsored by ILS Development and Training. A brief scientific report was also published in the ILS Research Journal.

The Rapid Earthquake Damage Assessment System (REDAS), a Geographical Information System (GIS) software has been used extensively throughout the study. It is a software which is used to provide a quick and near real-time simulated earthquake hazard map information and integrated with exposure data and risk elements for determining the extent of potential damage caused by a seismic hazard. The authors attempt to introduce the many capabilities of the software and how it can aid authorities in addressing common issues before, during and after an earthquake event.

REDAS is a free software and is continuously being upgraded as a result of other suggestions and inputs from authorities and users in the field.

The ultimate goal of this undertaking is to contribute to the various ways by which risk can be reduced to minimum levels and to be able to implement proper control measures and interventions before a known hazard becomes a disaster.

The authors greatly acknowledge the concepts and methodologies imparted to them by the team behind the birth of REDAS. Special mention should be made of the major contribution of Ma. Leonila P. Bautista through her presentations where Chapter III was based and to the Cagayan State University administration for the support given in the entire duration of this study. To our family for the moral and spiritual support – many thanks.

Policarpio L. Mabborang, Jr.
Juvylyn C. Amor

CHAPTER I

INTRODUCTION

The recent disasters that affect the world are alarming. The floods that result from typhoons and/or monsoon rains and the fires that literally would transform all tangibles into ashes, and the devastating effects of an earthquake are all valid reasons for everyone to stay alert. Reliable forecasts on the occurrence of such events are helpful in formulating safety measures to mitigate its consequences. New and state-of-art equipment along the field of meteorology now and again has been proven as a tool used by authorities to warn people of expected atmospheric disturbances that could result to excessive or limiting water that both has adverse effect on the general population. Despite advanced knowledge on the occurrence of these hydrological processes, significant damages still abound.

Today, the occurrence of earthquakes is still impossible to forecast although we know it will happen. If significant damages occur from natural disasters despite certain degrees of preparation to prevent the damages, moreso, if we are caught flat-footed!

An earthquake is a phenomenon that results from the sudden release of stored energy in the Earth's crust that creates seismic waves. At the Earth's surface, earthquakes may manifest themselves by a shaking or displacement of the ground and sometimes cause *tsunamis*, which may lead to loss of life and destruction of property. An earthquake is caused by tectonic plates (sections of the Earth's crust) getting stuck and putting a strain on the ground. The strain becomes so great that rocks give way and fault lines occur (http://en.wikipedia.org/ wiki/Earthquake).

In the Philippines, the Philippine Institute of Volcanology and Seismology (PHIVOLCS) of the Department of Science & Technology (DOST) is the mandated agency to mitigate disasters that may arise from such volcanic eruptions, earthquakes, *tsunamis*, and other related geotectonic phenomena. One of its modest attempts to help in this cause is the development of the Rapid Earthquake Damage Assessment System (REDAS), a Geographical Information System (GIS) software used to provide a quick and near real-time simulated earthquake hazard map information as well as integrated with exposure data and risk elements for determining the extent of potential damage caused by seismic hazard. The system is also supplemented with static hazard maps such as volcanic and hydro-meteorological, which expands its capability into multi-hazard approach. Its potential to be a risk assessment tool is being enhanced by improving the exposure database, inclusion of a building inventory module, incorporation of vulnerability curves and enhancing its modeling capability to address other natural hazards.

This study was funded by the Philippine Council for Industry, Engineering & Emerging Technology Research & Development (PCIEERD) of the DOST through the Regional Disaster Science and Management S & T Capacity Development Project. It utilized REDAS to evaluate the possible effects of an earthquake in the city of Tuguegarao, Cagayan. It only applied impact estimation and ground-shaking simulations on top of its many capabilities like landslide, liquefaction and tsunami forecasting.

The study area

Tuguegarao City, the capital of the Province of Cagayan and the Regional Center of Cagayan Valley (Region 02) is a major urban center in Northeastern Luzon and a Primary Growth

Center. Historically, it is important as the provincial capital of the Province of Cagayan; as a trading center for the Tobacco Monopoly; and as the only center for the higher education in Northeast Luzon (http://www.dotregion2.com.ph/d2/index.php?option=com_content&view=article&id=71&Itemid=83).

It has a total area of 144.80 km^2 and lies in the south central tip of the province. It is approximately 483 kilometers north of Manila, about 65 minutes by air travel and about 10 hours by land, through the Philippine-Japan Friendship Highway, also known as the Maharlika Highway, which is the region's trunk line road that which runs parallel to the Cagayan River. Tuguegarao City is bounded by Iguig, Cagayan on the north; by Peñablanca, Cagayan on the east; by the Province of Isabela on the south; and by the Cagayan River on the southwest and west. Across the river, the towns of Enrile and Solana are located to the southwest and west, respectively of Tuguegarao City. Using the Saint Peter's Cathedral Tower as landmark, the city's geographical coordinates are 121°43'46" longitude and 17°36'54" latitude. Its plain coordinates are 20,011.95 north and 20,106.67 east.

Tuguegarao City (Fig. 2) is composed of 49 barangays of which Carig Sur, Centro 6, and Centro 10 were chosen for the study. Carig Sur was chosen because it is the site of the regional center where the Cagayan Valley Medical Center (CVMC) and Cagayan State University-Carig campus are located which can be considered as the top (2) critical areas in the area.

A *barangay* is the basic political unit and the smallest administrative division in the Philippines (RA 7160: Local Government Code of the Philippines).

On the other hand, barangay Centro 6 has in its scope a commercial center, an elementary school, hotels, and a city hospital. Likewise, Centro 10 has two (2) places of worship (a mosque and the Sts. Peter & Paul cathedral). St. Peter and Paul metropolitan cathedral is the seat of the Archdiocese of Tuguegarao. The church with the belfry is the biggest Spanish-built church in Cagayan Valley constructed from January 17, 1761 to 1767. The cathedral suffered massive destruction in WWII and was later rebuilt by Msgr. Bishop Constance Jurgens. It is also characterized by commercial establishments, a hotel, the Cagayan provincial jail and a public park plus residential areas of different building typologies.

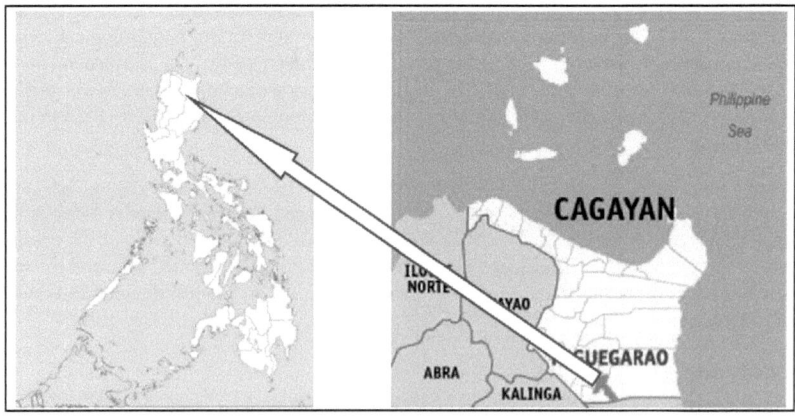

Fig. 1. Location site of the study area.

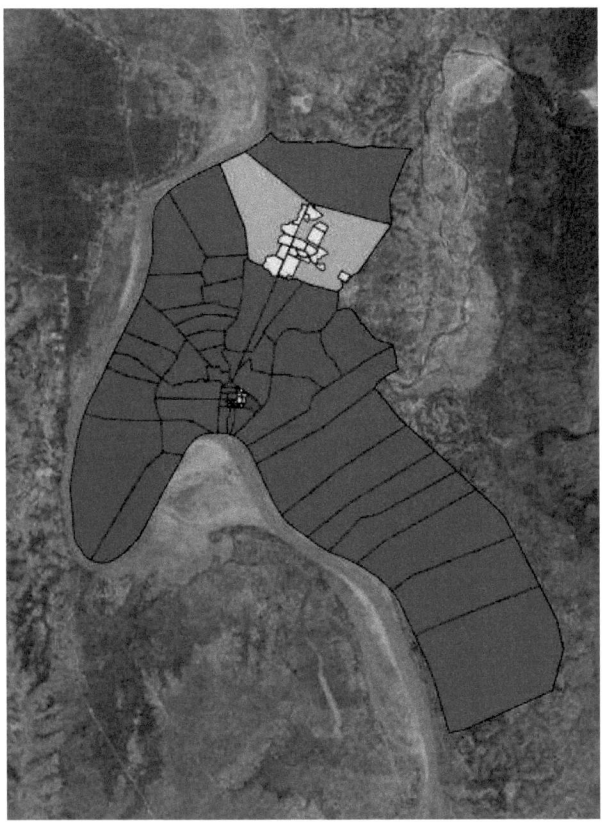

Fig. 2. Map of Tuguegarao City showing the pilot barangays (Carig Sur (topmost), Centro 6 (lower left), and Centro 10 (lower right)).

Historical earthquake events in Cagayan

The most recent observed earthquake event in Cagayan was in March 1, 2010. The center of the 6.1 magnitude tectonic quake was located 130 kilometers north-northeast of Tuguegarao City, with a depth of 21 kilometers (PHIVOLCS). A separate monitoring from the United States Geological Survey (USGS) puts the quake at magnitude 5.8 with a depth of 29 kilometers (http://www.sunstar.com.ph/ manila/61-magnitude-quake-rattles-tuguegarao). The highest recorded event (magnitude 8.0), however, was on November 30, 1619 off the north coast of Aparri, Cagayan (Fig.3).

The closest fault lines to the city is the one traversing the Sierra Madre mountain in Baggao, and another one running parallel to the Dummun river in Gattaran, Cagayan. On the north-west, another fault line has been identified from the municipality of Lasam towards Flora, Apayao province.

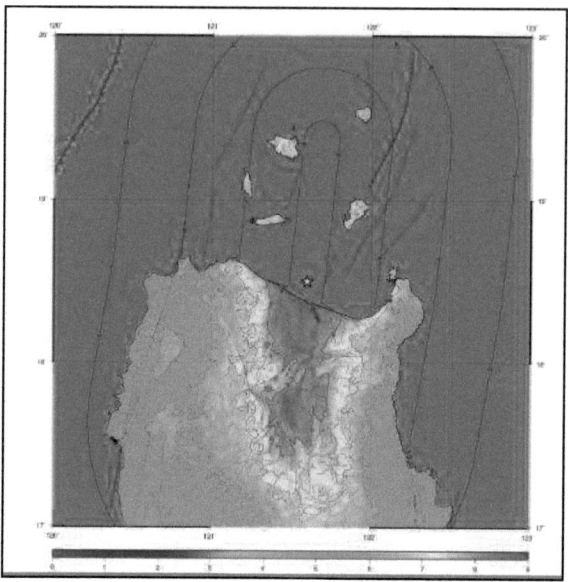

Fig. 3. Magnitude 8.0 earthquake off the north coast of Aparri, Cagayan on November 30, 1619.

Objectives of the study:

The overall objective of this study is to estimate earthquake risk using the Rapid Earthquake Damage Assessment System (REDAS).

Specifically it aims to:

- Develop earthquake exposure database;
- Estimate risks and calculate loss due to earthquake;
- Evaluate the capability of the Rapid Earthquake Damage Assessment System; and
- Provide local chief executives and legislators guidelines for policy formulation towards sound Disaster Risk Reduction (DRR) and related Climate Change Adaptation (CCA) initiatives.

CHAPTER II

REVIEW OF RELATED LITERATURE

The occurrence of earthquake is impossible to predict but we know one will occur. It is described by its magnitude which is measured using the Richter magnitude scale. It is a base-10 logarithmic scale. The magnitude is defined as the logarithm of the ratio of the amplitude of waves measured by a seismograph to an arbitrary small amplitude. An earthquake that measures 5.0 on the Richter scale has a shaking amplitude 10 times larger than one that measures 4.0, and corresponds to a 31.6 times larger release of energy (http://en.wikipedia.org/wiki/Richter_magnitude_scale). This implies that a magnitude 8.0 will be 31.6 x 31.6 more powerful than a magnitude 6.0 earthquake!

LIVESCIENCE shows the comparison of recent and historic earthquakes by energy release (shown in circles) in Fig. 4 below:

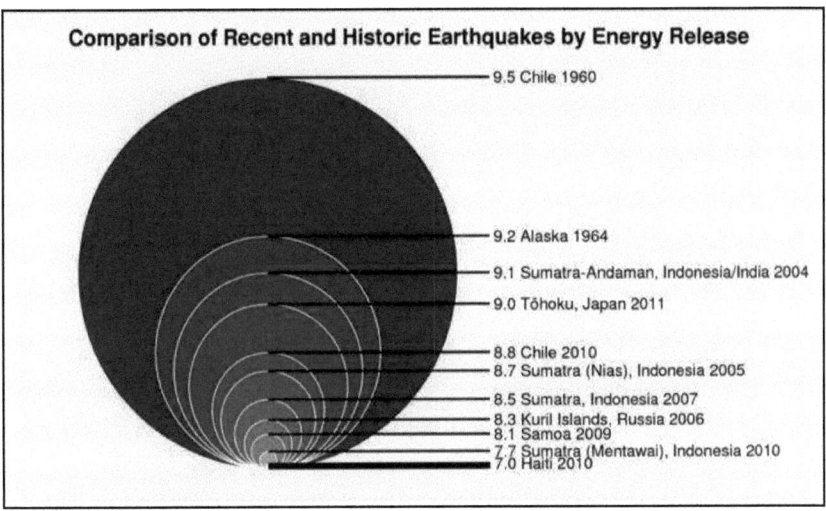

Fig. 4. Illustration showing the logarithmic relationship between one earthquake magnitude to another. (Cropped from LIVESCIENCE video on "Earthquake: What does magnitude mean?")

Intensity, on the other hand, measures the strength of shaking produced by the earthquake at a certain location. It is determined from effects on people, human structures, and the natural environment (http://earthquake.usgs.gov/learn/topics/mag_vs_int.php/10-22-2013). For practical purposes, PHIVOLCS provides the Earthquake Intensity Scale in Appendix 3 (Table A1). Same scale is also provided with caricatures for easier interpretation by local folks (reprinted February 2012).

We can never predict when an earthquake is going to strike, but we can certainly take some precautionary measures, before and after an earthquake, thus minimizing the damage caused by it.

Philippines is within the Pacific Ring of Fire which makes it vulnerable to earthquakes. Fig. 5 shows the historic earthquake events based on NEIC data. This however, does not mean that there is reason to panic. There are many parts of the world like Japan where earthquakes occur very frequently, but there is little or no loss of life or damage to property, as the people have learned to live with them. They have constructed earthquake-safe buildings and practice the Do's and Don'ts (Ali, 2008) regarding earthquakes (http://www.merinews.com/article/earthquake-safety-measures/131229.shtml/ 10/22/13).

Vulnerability is a function of exposure, susceptibility and coping capacity, focusing on social, economic and environmental and dimensions (Kamiri et al, 2010). Risk, on the other hand is the product of a given vulnerability and a certain hazard. Hazards become disasters when vulnerable conditions exist among people, resources and other elements are exposed to risk, and capacity/measures to cope with consequences are insufficient.

The first generation of catastrophe models built exclusively for the insurance industry emerged in the late 1980s (Risk Management Solutions, Inc., 2009). These models represent the decades-long culmination of research on the science of natural hazards, the response of structures to ground motion, and the quantitative measurement of risk—in essence, the synthesis of multidisciplinary efforts from scientific researchers, structural engineers, actuaries, and other financial statisticians. For earthquake hazard, much of this research was centered on earthquake risk in the United States, although researchers across the globe contributed to the birth of the catastrophe modeling industry.

In the Philippines, the Metro Manila Earthquake Impact Reduction Study (MMEIRS) estimates that 38,000 people will be killed and more than 100,000 will be injured if a magnitude 7.2 earthquake will hit Metro Manila. This event may happen anytime from now though it is said that this has a return period of 200 years. In fact, the Metro Manila Development Authority (MMDA) in coordination with PHIVOLCS and some agencies have conducted an earthquake drill in preparation for what authorities call "The Big One". The big one is the anticipated 7.2 magnitude quake that may occur in the East and West Valley Faults that traverse the Metro Manila area and nearby provinces. The megaquake will also topple at least 13 percent of the 170,000 residential buildings and will leave 1.2 million people homeless. It can also damage 20 percent of the vital facilities such as hospitals, government centers and schools (Philippine Daily Inquirer, June 8, 2013 issue).

Recently, however, the high degree of unpredictability of the frequency of occurrence has been demonstrated by the two (2) consecutive earthquakes in Nepal in a matter of less than three weeks. Magnitude 7.8 happened on April 25, 2015 resulting to 8,857 officially dead and 21, 952 injured (https://en.wikipedia.org/wiki/April_2015_Nepal_earthquake/August_18, 2015) while another magnitude 7.3 on May 12, 2015 resulted to 218 dead and 3,500 injured (https://en.wikipedia.org/wiki/May_2015_Nepal_earthquake/August_18, 2015).

Another similar study by PHIVOLCS reveals what it said would be the worst case scenario of a magnitude 7.2 earthquake that can be generated by valley fault system, which runs lengthwise along the National Capital Region. Based on this study, an event like this will trigger an intensity 8.0 earthquake in the Greater Metro Manila area and around 37,000 deaths are expected, and the estimated damage is at P2.5 trillion (http://www.abs-cbnnews.com/nation/metro-manila/10/17/13/magnitude-72-quake-metro-manila-will-kill-37000)

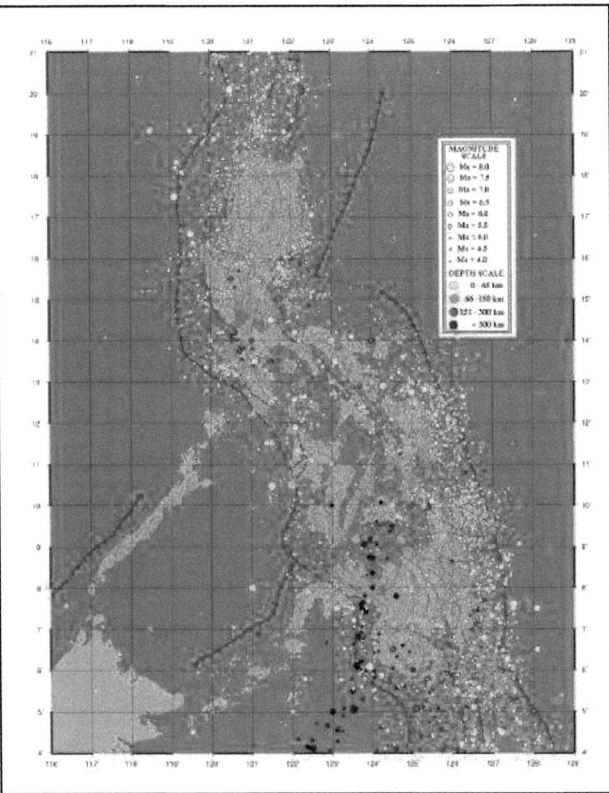

Fig. 5. Philippine seismicity map.

As a safety measure, proper monitoring and implementation of the updated National Building Code of the Philippines (2010) must be required of all local government units. On top of this, Section 421 of the National Structural Code of the Philippines (2010) provides the requirements for earthquake resistant structures as a preventive measure to curb the possible effects of a tremor due to structural failure.

PHIVOLCS-DOST team has developed Rapid Earthquake Damage Assessment System (REDAS) - a software which is intended to show near-real time scenario of an earthquake. It is an integrated system that considers building typologies, location, (see Appendix 1) and some details of the earthquake event to come up with effects to immediate and nearby locations. In 2012, Lanuza used REDAS in a case study for landuse planning specifically to the vulnerability of Gabaldon, Nueva Ecija to earthquake hazards. Lately, REDAS was used to generate the areal extent of the earthquake that struck Bohol last October 20, 2013 (Fig. 6).

In addition, the Federal Emergency Management Agency (FEMA), United States of America (2011) explains the sources of nonstructural earthquake damage and provides methods for reducing potential risks since nonstructural failures have accounted for the majority of

7

earthquake damage in several recent U.S. earthquakes. It addresses nonstructural components of a building, which include all of those components that are not part of the structural system; that is, all of the architectural, mechanical, electrical, and plumbing systems, as well as furniture, fixtures, equipment, and contents.

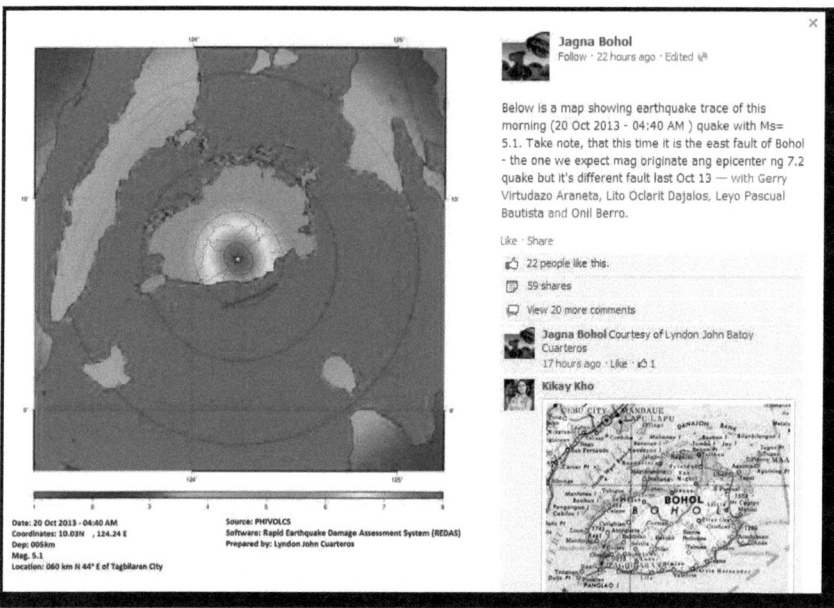

Fig. 6. Intensity map generated for magnitude 5.1 earthquake at 4:40 AM of October 20, 2013 at Bohol Province using REDAS (Facebook.com/10-21-2013)

Despite the existence of these models, it is still considered best to take measures to safeguard both populations and properties against potential damage, death and destruction by pooling resources together and identifying concrete steps from planning, development, and proper implementation of policies and programs towards this end.

CHAPTER III

REDAS: An Overview

Conceptual Framework

This section has been synthesized from presentations conducted by Baustista (2014) during a training on the use of REDAS in the province of Cagayan, Philippines. It includes among others the basic concepts and principles used in the development of the software. The equations used in coming up with the damage forecasts, economic loss and casualties are presented in detail along with reference or look-up tables.

REDAS as a risk assessment tool:

ISO/IEC Guide 73 (2002) prominently defines risk as *a combination of the probability of an event and its consequence.... when there is at least the possibility of negative consequences*. Technically speaking, it involves determining the hazard involved; the exposure (elements at risk); and their vulnerability.

$$Risk = hazard \; x \; exposure \; x \; vulnerability$$

The nature of the hazard can be taken from hazard maps prepared from concerned agencies using different appropriate models. Hazard is a phenomenon, event, or occurrence that has the potential for causing injury or damage to life or property or to the environment These can be geologic or hydro-meteorologic in nature. Earthquake for example, is a natural phenomenon that can be very damaging depending on the amount of energy released during the event. To compound the problem, there is still no means yet by which its occurrence can be predicted and where it may happen - although we all know that will happen.

Exposure on the other hand involves the elements-at-risk that may be damaged or injured should a particular hazard occur like the people, buildings, infrastructure, and lifeline utilities that lie within a hazard footprint.

A comprehensive exposure database contains information on the following:

- spatial location of people and structures (including residential, business, emergency services and critical infrastructure);
- construction information including material type (e.g., wall and roof type), number of stories and vintage; and
- value of structures and contents.

In 1994, Harris (as cited by Bautista, 2014) has clearly compared these two terms in a caricature as shown in Fig. 7.

Similarly, vulnerability refers to the conditions determined by physical, social, economic, and environmental factors or processes, which increase the susceptibility of a community to the impact of hazards. On the physical aspect, this may involve equations that simulate the existing conditions thereby giving a close estimate to what might be expected once a hazard occurs to a given set of elements directly or indirectly exposed. On the part of administrators or local chief executives, the known vulnerabilities of a given area can serve as bases in formulating counter-measures to increase the capacity of the community and social institutions to properly address immediate issues during and after a given event to curb negative consequences. Among these include proper engineering designs to withstand certain degrees of hazards and information dissemination to make people aware of the "Do's and Don'ts" in case of emergency.

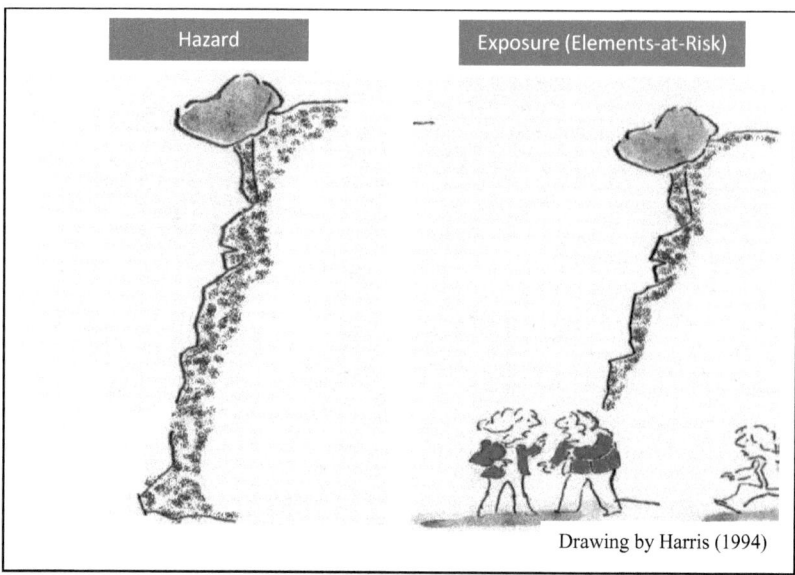

Fig. 7. Comparison between hazard and exposure (Harris, 1994).

The Philippine Institute of Volcanology and Seismology (PHIVOLCS) of the Department of Science & Technology (Philippines), is the mandated agency to mitigate disasters that may arise from such volcanic eruptions, earthquakes, tsunamis, and other related geotectonic phenomena. In its bid to attain its objectives as embodied in its mission and goals, the agency has formed a team to spearhead the development of a risk assessment tool that would integrate location-specific information on the susceptibility to damages as a result of strong tremors.

The Rapid Earthquake Damage Assessment System (REDAS) is a Geographical Information System (GIS) software used to provide a quick and near real-time simulated earthquake hazard map information as well as integrated with exposure data and risk elements for determining the extent of potential damage caused by seismic hazard. The system is also supplemented with static hazard maps such as volcanic and hydro-meteorological, which expands its capability into multi-hazard approach. Its potential to be a risk assessment tool is being enhanced by improving the exposure database, inclusion of a building inventory module, incorporation of vulnerability curves and enhancing its modeling capability to address other natural hazards.

To date, the software is equipped with possibilities to estimate earthquake impact to physical damages, fatalities in the affected area, and corresponding economic loss. It is being continuously upgraded to include suggestions from end-users and other authorities like geologists, engineers, planners, and policy makers. It is regretful, however, that the system was built under Philippine setting only. With similar data requirements from other countries, the software though could be worked-out to make it applicable where similar studies and research endeavors are wanted.

How does REDAS works?

The following section will discuss briefly the concepts and principles applied in making estimates in terms of physical damages, fatalities and injuries, and economic loss in an earthquake-stricken area. The results may be in table form, GIS shapefiles, or in REDAS plot files.

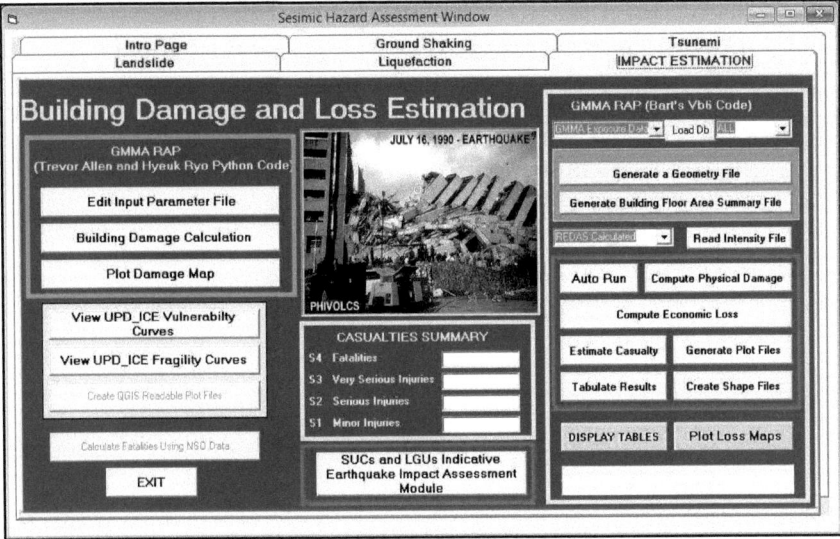

Fig. 8. Building damage and loss estimation module of REDAS.

a. Physical damages

The physical damages that a building structure may incur after being subjected to a given seismic motion varies according to the amount of energy released and the building attributes to withstand the shaking motion. These are subdivided into five levels namely:

i. Slight Damage
ii. Moderate Damage
iii. Extensive Damage
iv. Complete Damage with NO collapse
v. Complete Damage with collapse

Required Inputs for Computing Physical Damage

1. Ground Shaking Hazard Map (must use Modified Mercalli Intensity (MMI) Scale)
2. Exposure Database (landuse-derived, National Statistics Office (NSO) or survey data)
3. Fragility and Vulnerability Curves → Developed by UPD-ICE

Before proceeding further to the next steps, it is assumed that the user has fully understood the simple techniques and basic modules on how to use REDAS. If not, then user is advised to consult the REDAS Manual.

Step 1:

Determine level of intensity in your chosen study area. Assume that the highest magnitude earthquake ever recorded in the area will occur again and simulate the resulting earthquake intensity. Generate your own map using REDAS software.

Step 2:

Derive exposure data for your study area using landuse-derived, barangay-level NSO or survey data. Data needed include:

a. Total floor area (for 18 building types)
b. Predominant Era of Construction
c. Population/building type/barangay

Table 1. The 18 Building Types with earthquake fragility and vulnerability curves as generated by UPD-ICE:

W1 L	C1 L	S1 L
W3 L	C1 M	S1 M
CHB L	C4 M	S3 L
URA L	C4 H	S4 M
URA M	PC2 L	MWS L
CSW L	C2 M	N L

a) Sample of land use exposure information for risk assessment

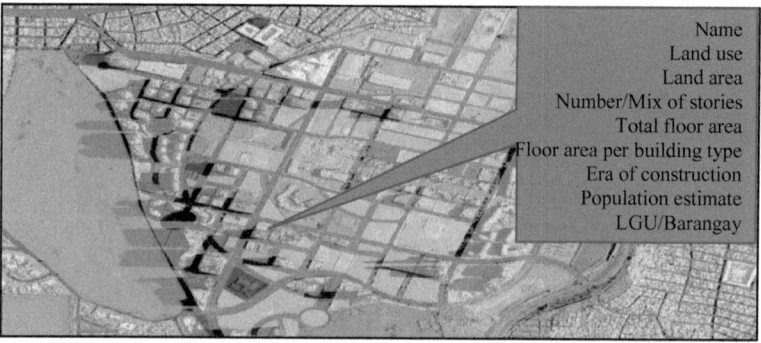

Name
Land use
Land area
Number/Mix of stories
Total floor area
Floor area per building type
Era of construction
Population estimate
LGU/Barangay

b) Barangay-level Exposure Database from NSO data

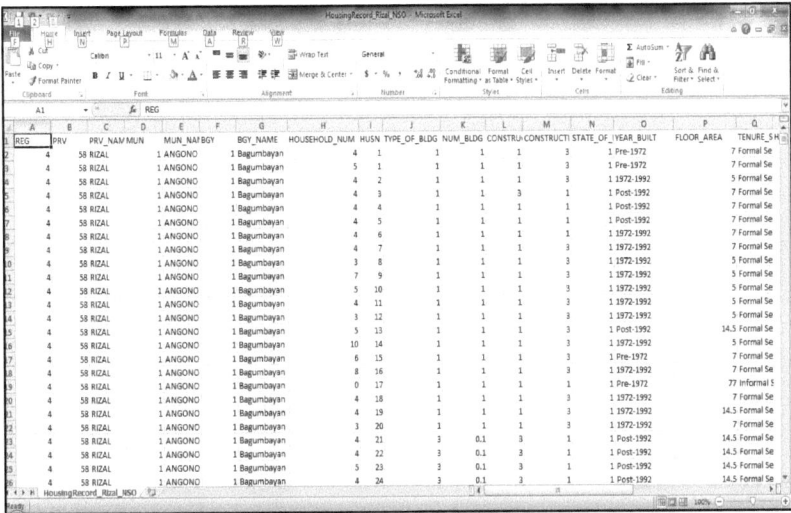

c) Building Survey using REDAS Exposure Database

Exposure Database Module (EDM) windows: This contains approximately 100 questions related to buildings. For complete details of these information, see Appendix 1.

1.Green Window Opening Menu – Geographic Information.	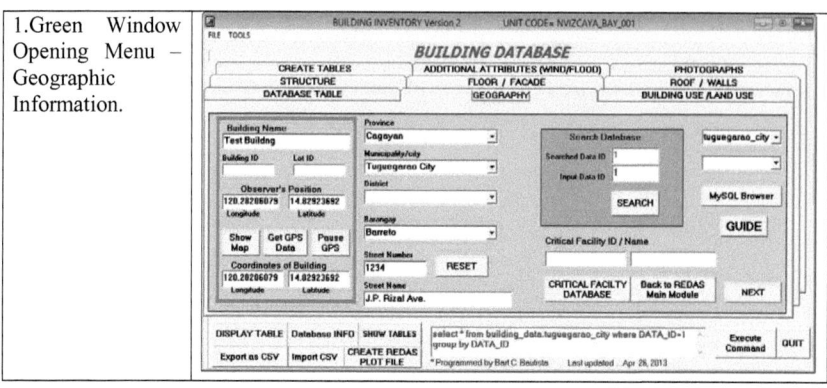
2.Cyan Window – Building Use	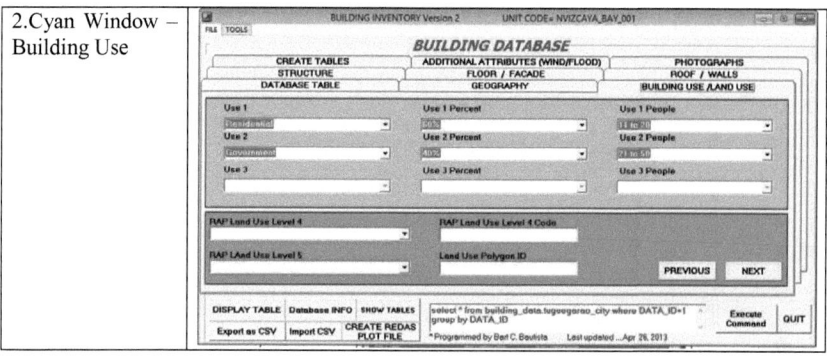
3.Teal Window – Roof and Walls Data	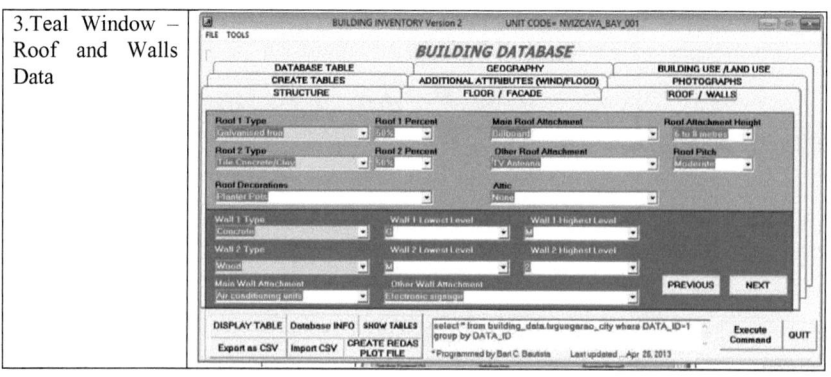

4.Orange Window – Floor and Façade	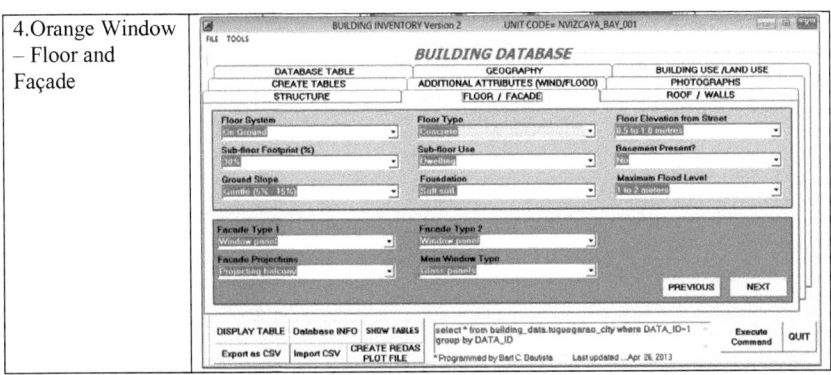
5.Yellow Window –Structural Information	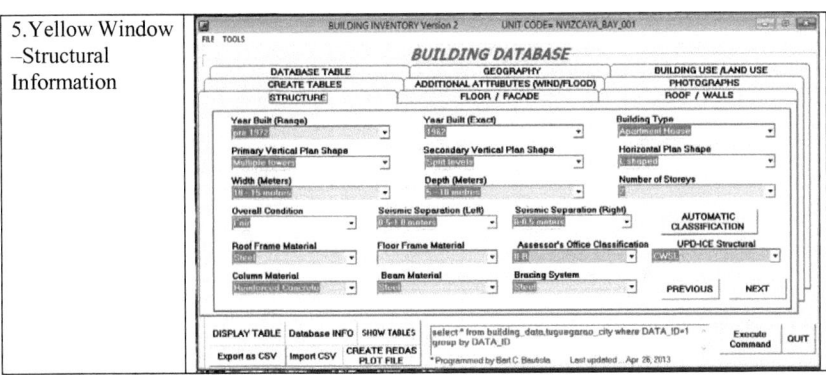
6.Red Window – Attributes for Wind and Flood	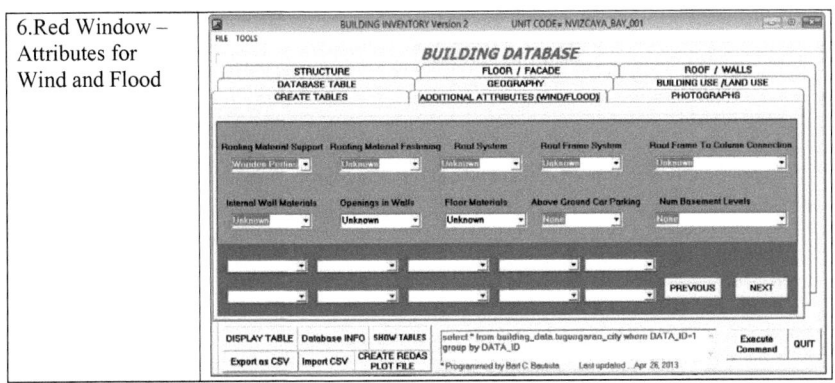

7.Pink Window – Photographs, Data Appending, Other Comments	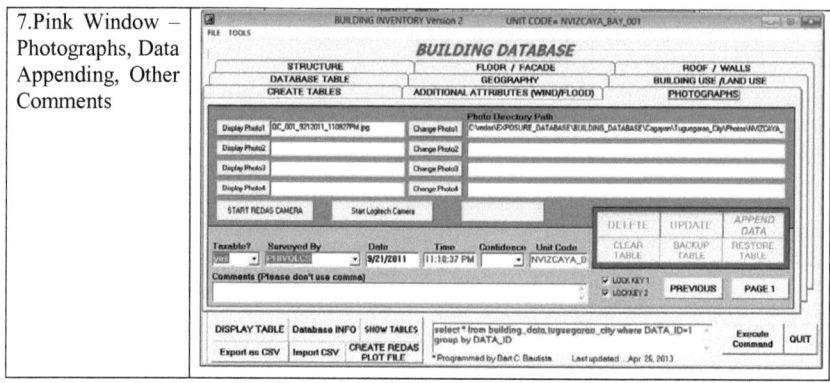

REDAS GPS Field Survey Form

Points

Bldg No.	Bldg Name	Longi tude °	Latitu de °	Length (m)	Width (m)	No. of Floors	Bldg Class	Era of Construc tion	No. of Occu pants	Bldg Value	Current Value	Landuse 4 code	Landuse 5 code	Photo file
Sam ple		120.90 47	15.71 166	20	12	2	C1	Post 1992	6	1 millio n	500,00 0	1	1.1	Num ber.jp g
1														
2														
3														
4														
5														
6														
7														
8														
9														
10														

Fragility and Vulnerability Curves

We can determine the probability of physical damage whether these are for complete, extensive, moderate and slight damages from the fragility curves. For each building type and construction era, use the intensity level to determine the probability of being in a certain damage state.

Note: The earthquake fragility curves describe the likelihood of physical damage for a range of different building types.

How to interpret the fragility curves:

Fig. 9 shows a sample window used in conducting earthquake building fragility computation. Confirmation of the appropriate parameters from the pull-down menus in the left and bottom sides of the window and making sure that each time a new set of analysis and computation is conducted the graphs must be cleared.

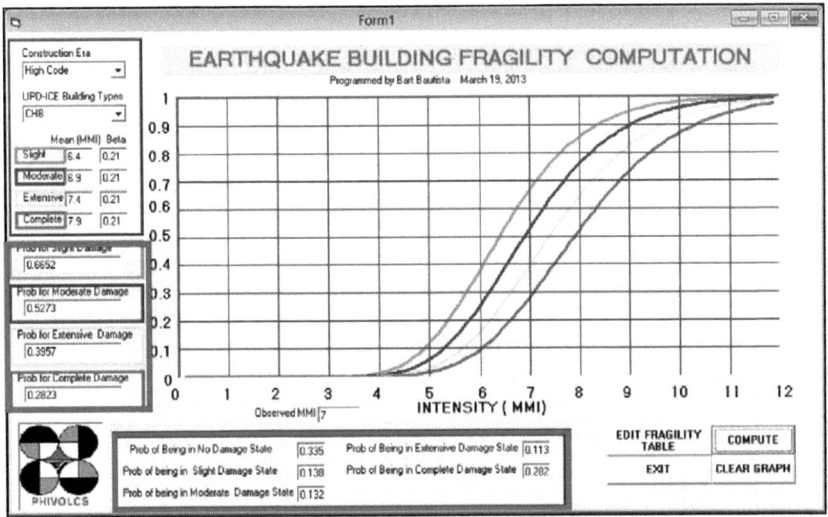

Fig. 9. Typical fragility curve with the different parameters as indicated in the pull-down menus.

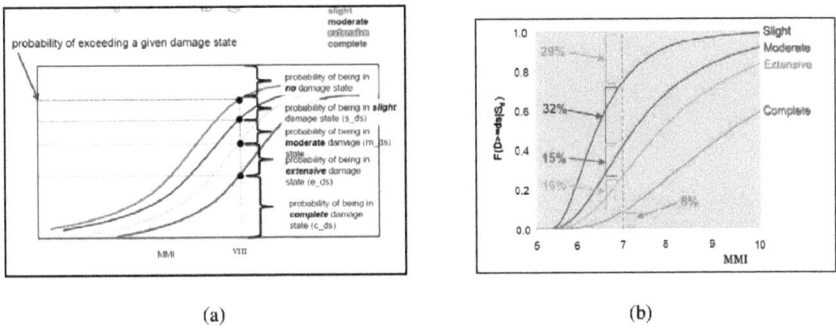

Fig. 10 a & b. Breaking down the fragility curve into corresponding probabilities (earthquake intensity-related).

For the typical curve shown in Fig. 9 above, the probabilities for slight damage, moderate damage, extensive damage and complete damage can be read directly from the color-coded boxes (highlighted in red box) in the left side whose values can also be confirmed by looking at the corresponding values to the left of the respective color-coded curves. The working equations, though, require the probability "of being in a given damage state". These values are readily available at the lower (red) box indicating thereat the different damage states. Likewise, these same values can be computed manually using the following equations:

> ➤ Probability of being in No Damage State = 1.0 – Probability for Slight Damage
> ➤ Probability of being in Slight Damage State = Probability for Slight Damage – Probability for Moderate Damage

17

➢ Probability of being in Moderate Damage State = Probability for Moderate Damage –
Probability for Extensive Damage
➢ Probability of being in Extensive Damage State = Probability for Extensive Damage –
Probabilty for Complete Damage
➢ Probability of being in Complete Damage State = Probabilty for Complete Damage

Step 3: Computing for Physical Damage: Get the Total Floor Area (TFA) for a given Damage
State for a Land Use or for Barangay

Working equations:

$Building\_TFA_{c\_ds}$ = $Building\ Type_{TFA}$ × $Probability\ "of\ being\ in\ a\ damage\ state"_{c\_ds}$
$Building\_TFA_{e\_ds}$ = $Building\ Type_{TFA}$ × $Probability\ "of\ being\ in\ a\ damage\ state"_{e\_ds}$
$Building\_TFA_{m\_ds}$ = $Building\ Type_{TFA}$ × $Probability\ "of\ being\ in\ a\ damage\ state"_{m\_ds}$
$Building\_TFA_{s\_ds}$ = $Building\ Type_{TFA}$ × $Probability\ "of\ being\ in\ a\ damage\ state"_{s\_ds}$

        from Exposure data   from fragility curves for a given intensity level

TFA - total floor area c_ds - complete damage state
e_ds - extensive damage state m_ds - moderate damage state
s_ds - slight damage state

Step 4: Complete damage (cd_s) is divided into Complete Collapse (cc) and Complete with
NO collapse (cn)

Working equation for Complete Damage state:

• Complete Collapse (cc)
• Complete with no collapse (cn)

$Building\_TFA_{cc} = Building\_TFA_{c\_ds}$ × $Building\ collapse\ rate$

           From step 3   from collapse rate look-up table

TFA - total floor area   c_ds - complete damage state
cc - complete damage with collapse   cn - complete damage with no collapse

Step 5: For complete damage with no collapse, use the following equation and refer to
collapse_rate Look up Table

Working equation: Complete Damage NO Collapse (cn)

$Building\_TFA_{cn} = Building\_TFA_{c\_ds} - Building\_TFA_{cc}$

          From step 3   from step 4

W1 L,CHB L, W3 L, etc   - building types
TFA   - total floor area
c-ds   - complete damage state
cc   - complete damage with collapse
cn   - complete damage with no collapse

Table 2. Collapse_rate Look-up Table:

HAZUS	PHIL BUILDING_TYPE	Collapse rate for complete structural damage
W1	W1 L	0.03
W1	W3 L	0.03
W1	N L	0.03
URM L	MWS L	0.15
URM L	CHB L	0.15
URM L	URA L	0.15
URM L	URM L	0.15
URM L	CWS L	0.15
C1 L	C1 L	0.13
C1 M	C1 M	0.1
C1 M	C4 M	0.1
C1 H	C4 H	0.05
PC2 L	PC2 L	0.15
PC2 M	PC2 M	0.13
S1 L	S1 L	0.08
S1 M	S1 M	0.05
S3	S3 L	0.03
S4 M	S4 M	0.05

NSO exposure data:

Look-up table to correlate NSO wall-roof combinations to UPD-ICE building classification:

Roof type		Wall type	
1	Galvanized Iron/Aluminum	1	Concrete/Brick/Stone
2	Tile Concrete/Clay Tile	2	Wood
3	Half Galvanized Iron And Half Concrete	3	Half Concrete/Brick/Stone And Half Wood
4	Wood	4	Galvanized Iron/Aluminum
5	Cogon/Nipa/Anahaw	5	Bamboo/Sawali/Cogon/Nipa
6	Asbestos	6	Asbestos
7	Makeshift/Salvaged/Improvised Materials	7	Glass
		8	Makeshift/Salvaged/Improvised Materials
8	Others	9	Others
		10	No Walls
9	Not Reported	99	Not Reported

NSO Roof Wall	W1	W3	N	CHB	URA	URM	MWS	CWS	C1	S1	S3
1_1				35%					65%		
1_2	100%										
1_3							35%	65%			
1_4			80%								20%
1_5		100%									
1_6	100%										

19

b. Fatalities and injuries

Step 1: Get occupancy rate (OR):

$$OR = \frac{total\ population\ of\ household}{total\ floor\ area\ of\ each\ building\ type}$$

Casualties may be further subdivided according to the degree of injuries that the residents may incur:

i.   Slight Injuries (S1)
ii.   Non-life threatening injuries (S2)
iii.   Life Threatening injuries (S3)
iv.   Fatalities (S4)

Step 2: Compute for the four (4) casualty levels (S1 to S4) for the five physical damage states for the 18 building types

Example: Slight Injuries (S1) for complete collapse (TFAcc):

$$S1\_Building_{cc} = Building\_TFA_{cc} \times OR \times Buildings\_{S1}$$

⬆   ⬆

From step 4   from casualty rate look-up table

Table 3. Brief description of the different injury levels that may be incurred by affected residents during an earthquake.

Injury severity level	Description
1	Injuries requiring basic medical aid that could be administered by paraprofessionals. These types of injuries would require bandages or observation. Some examples include sprain, a severe cut requiring stitches, a minor burn (first degree or second degree on a small part of the body), or a bump on the head without loss of consciousness. Injuries of lesser severity that could be self treated are not estimated by HAZUS.
2	Injuries requiring a greater degree of medical care and use of medical technology such as x-rays or surgery, but not expected to progress to a life threatening status. Some examples are third degree burns or second degree burns over large parts of the body, a bump on the head that causes loss of consciousness, fractured bone, dehydration or exposure.
3	Injuries that pose an immediate life threatening condition if not treated adequately and expeditiously. These may involve uncontrolled bleeding, punctured organ, other internal injuries, spinal column injuries, or crush syndrome.
4	Instantaneously killed or mortally injured.

Computing for S1 to S4 for five physical damage for building:

$S1\_Building_{cc} = Building\_TFA_{cc} \times OR \times Building_{cc\_s1}$
$S1\_Building_{nc} = Building\_TFA_{nc} \times OR \times Building_{nc\_s1}$
$S1\_Building_{e\_ds} = Building\_TFA_{e\_ds} \times OR \times Building_{e\_s1}$
$S1\_Building_{m\_ds} = Building\_TFA_{m\_ds} \times OR \times Building_{m\_s1}$
$S1\_Building_{s\_ds} = Building\_TFA_{s\_ds} \times OR \times Building_{s\_s1}$

Slight
Injuries

S1

$S2\_Building_{cc} = Building\_TFA_{cc} \times OR \times Building_{cc\_s2}$
$S2\_Building_{nc} = Building\_TFA_{nc} \times OR \times Building_{nc\_s2}$
$S2\_Building_{e\_ds} = Building\_TFA_{e\_ds} \times OR \times Building_{e\_s2}$
$S2\_Building_{m\_ds} = Building\_TFA_{m\_ds} \times OR \times Building_{m\_s2}$
$S2\_Building_{s\_ds} = Building\_TFA_{s\_ds} \times OR \times Building_{s\_s2}$

Non-life
threatening
injuries

S2

$S3\_Building_{cc} = Building\_TFA_{cc} \times OR \times Building_{cc\_s3}$
$S3\_Building_{nc} = Building\_TFA_{nc} \times OR \times Building_{nc\_s3}$
$S3\_Building_{e\_ds} = Building\_TFA_{e\_ds} \times OR \times Building_{e\_s3}$
$S3\_Building_{m\_ds} = Building\_TFA_{m\_ds} \times OR \times Building_{m\_s3}$
$S3\_Building_{s\_ds} = Building\_TFA_{s\_ds} \times OR \times Building_{s\_s3}$

Life
threatening
injuries

S3

$S4\_Building_{cc} = Building\_TFA_{cc} \times OR \times Building_{cc\_s4}$
$S4\_Building_{nc} = Building\_TFA_{nc} \times OR \times Building_{nc\_s4}$
$S4\_Building_{e\_ds} = Building\_TFA_{e\_ds} \times OR \times Building_{e\_s4}$
$S4\_Building_{m\_ds} = Building\_TFA_{m\_ds} \times OR \times Building_{m\_s4}$
$S4\_Building_{s\_ds} = Building\_TFA_{s\_ds} \times OR \times Building_{s\_s4}$

Fatalities

S4

Table 4. HAZUS Casualty Rate Look-up Table:

UPD-ICE	HAZUS	S_S1	S_S2	S_S3	S_S4	M_S1	M_S2	M_S3	M_S4	E_S1	E_S2	E_S3	E_S4	CN_S1	CN_S2	CN_S3	CN_S4	CC_S1	CC_S2	CC_S3	CC_S4
W1L	W1	0.0005	0	0	0	0.0025	0.0003	0	0	0.01	0.001	0.00001	0.00001	0.05	0.01	0.0001	0.0001	0.4	0.2	0.03	0.05
W3L	W1	0.0005	0	0	0	0.0025	0.0003	0	0	0.01	0.001	0.00001	0.00001	0.05	0.01	0.0001	0.0001	0.4	0.2	0.03	0.05
NL	W1	0.0005	0	0	0	0.0025	0.0003	0	0	0.01	0.001	0.00001	0.00001	0.05	0.01	0.0001	0.0001	0.4	0.2	0.03	0.05
MWSL	URML	0.0005	0	0	0	0.0035	0.0004	0.00001	0.00001	0.02	0.002	0.00002	0.00002	0.1	0.02	0.0002	0.0002	0.4	0.2	0.05	0.1
CHBL	URML	0.0005	0	0	0	0.0035	0.0004	0.00001	0.00001	0.02	0.002	0.00002	0.00002	0.1	0.02	0.0002	0.0002	0.4	0.2	0.05	0.1
URAL	URML	0.0005	0	0	0	0.0035	0.0004	0.00001	0.00001	0.02	0.002	0.00002	0.00002	0.1	0.02	0.0002	0.0002	0.4	0.2	0.05	0.1
URML	URML	0.0005	0	0	0	0.0035	0.0004	0.00001	0.00001	0.02	0.002	0.00002	0.00002	0.1	0.02	0.0002	0.0002	0.4	0.2	0.05	0.1
CWSL	URML	0.0005	0	0	0	0.0035	0.0004	0.00001	0.00001	0.02	0.002	0.00002	0.00002	0.1	0.02	0.0002	0.0002	0.4	0.2	0.05	0.1
C1L	C1L	0.0005	0	0	0	0.0025	0.0003	0	0	0.01	0.001	0.00001	0.00001	0.05	0.01	0.0001	0.0001	0.4	0.2	0.05	0.1
C1M	C1M	0.0005	0	0	0	0.0025	0.0003	0	0	0.01	0.001	0.00001	0.00001	0.05	0.01	0.0001	0.0001	0.4	0.2	0.05	0.1
C4M	C1M	0.0005	0	0	0	0.0025	0.0003	0	0	0.01	0.001	0.00001	0.00001	0.05	0.01	0.0001	0.0001	0.4	0.2	0.05	0.1
C4H	C1H	0.0005	0	0	0	0.0025	0.0003	0	0	0.01	0.001	0.00001	0.00001	0.05	0.01	0.0001	0.0001	0.4	0.2	0.05	0.1
PC2L	PC2L	0.0005	0	0	0	0.0025	0.0003	0	0	0.01	0.001	0.00001	0.00001	0.05	0.01	0.0001	0.0001	0.4	0.2	0.05	0.1
PC2M	PC2M	0.0005	0	0	0	0.0025	0.0003	0	0	0.01	0.001	0.00001	0.00001	0.05	0.01	0.0001	0.0001	0.4	0.2	0.05	0.1
S1L	S1L	0.0005	0	0	0	0.002	0.00025	0	0	0.01	0.001	0.00001	0.00001	0.05	0.01	0.0001	0.0001	0.4	0.2	0.05	0.1
S1M	S1M	0.0005	0	0	0	0.002	0.00025	0	0	0.01	0.001	0.00001	0.00001	0.05	0.01	0.0001	0.0001	0.4	0.2	0.05	0.1
S3L	S3	0.0005	0	0	0	0.002	0.00025	0	0	0.01	0.001	0.00001	0.00001	0.05	0.01	0.0001	0.0001	0.4	0.2	0.03	0.05
S4M	S4M	0.0005	0	0	0	0.002	0.0003	0	0	0.01	0.001	0.00001	0.00001	0.05	0.01	0.0001	0.0001	0.4	0.2	0.05	0.1

Step 3: Sum all casualty levels (S1, S2, S3, S4) for ALL damage states for ALL building types

Example:

$S1 = S1\_Building_{cc} + S1\_Building_{nc} + S1\_Building_{e\_ds} + S1\_Building_{m\_ds} + S1\_Building_{s\_ds}$

Do the same (S1 to S4) for all five (5) damage states for all the 18 building types.

c. Economic loss

Vulnerability curves describe the loss ratio (i.e. ratio of repair cost to building replacement value) as a function of the ground shaking for a range of different building types. For example, a loss ratio of 0.5 means that the cost of repairing the damaged building is equal to 50% of its replacement cost.

Loss ratio are derived from vulnerability curves. The curve depends on building type, predominant era of construction, earthquake intensity (Fig. 11).

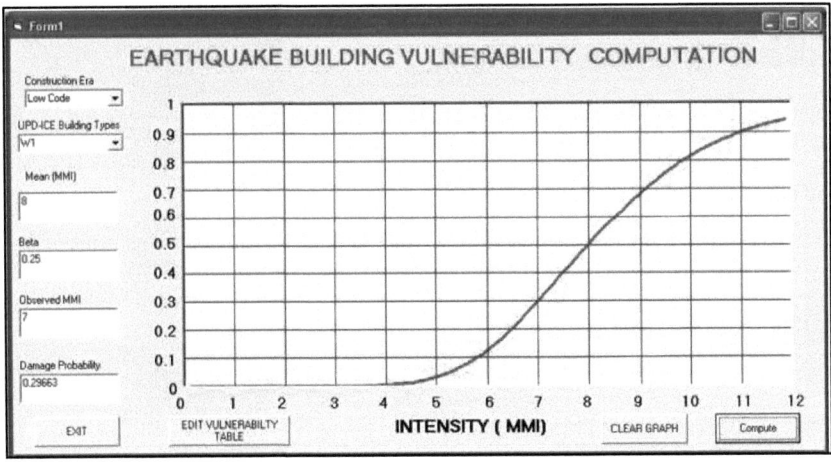

Fig. 11. Sample vulnerability curve for a building made up of wood (W1) constructed before 1974 (Low Code) subjected to an earthquake with observed MMI of 7.0. Same building is expected to have a damage probability of 0.29663.

Regular software upgrading:

The team behind the development of the software is regularly exploring all possibilities to improve and upgrade its capabilities. Two versions were used in this study to emphasize the great improvement attained as a result of suggestions and recommendations from authorities along the field of earthquake study and from disaster risk reduction management personnel.

For other inquiries and suggestions, the reader may feel free to contact the Philippine Institute of Volcanology and Seismology (PHIVOLCS-DOST) at http://www.phivolcs.dost.gov.ph.

CHAPTER IV

METHODOLOGY

Capacity Building

Training on the use of the REDAS was conducted at the Central Luzon State University (CLSU) at the Science City of Munoz, Nueva Ecija. Familiarity with Quantum GIS (QGIS) software is also equally important. This involved participants from cooperating State Universities and Colleges from three different pilot regions in the country. Enumerators were also briefed with proper techniques in the conduct of the survey.

Site selection and survey proper

As stated earlier, (3) barangays were chosen for the study. A questionnaire was prepared out of the Building Inventory module of REDAS which include among others the building use, structure, period built, geography, and estimated number of occupants. Prior to field immersion for actual data gathering, a permit from the local government unit (Appendix 2a & 2b)) was first secured to avoid problems. Proper coordination with barangay officials was also done and relevant information about the barangay was obtained. Temporary ID's were issued to enumerators for proper identification.

Where requested, specific communications were addressed to agency heads for permission to conduct the study within their jurisdiction

Exposure Database

The major output of the study is the exposure database for every location which is important. It shows the elements at risk that lie within a hazard footprint like ground shaking from an earthquake. Among the information that can be extracted from the database are those shown in the questionnaire (Appendix 1).

Three separate exposure maps was generated for the pilot barangays.

Land Use Polygons and Building Statistics

QGIS was used in delineating the landuse polygons for the three (3) barangays. In each of the pilot barangays, blocks with common landuse are considered as one. To facilitate easier interpretation, legends are provided in each map. Actual landuse is also matched with the existing Landuse Plan of the City (Appendix 4). This is important especially in the generation of earthquake risks maps. Information generated from the exposure database module is integrated with the REDAS and QGIS programs.

Risk Calculation and Loss Estimation

There are equations in the REDAS program used to calculate risk and estimate loss due to earthquakes. The fragility curves developed by UP-Institute of Civil Engineering as integrated by the system was also adapted.

To obtain realistic estimates of damages, existing average cost of construction for the dominant types of structures was used. This represents the replacement cost for the damaged structures once they are being erected again.

With the use of the updated version of the software, however, estimates of the expected effects like injuries, fatalities, and economic loss was also generated both using data from actual survey and from the National Statistics Office (NSO) of the Philippines.

Chapter III discusses briefly some of the key points considered in the calculation procedures and estimates.

Paintbrushing

Paintbrushing is a technique used to extrapolate the risk and loss estimates from actual survey data and NSO data taken from a localized sample study area to a wider scope. It assumes that the sampling study in the three (3) barangays chosen are close representations of the other remaining areas and that they are all subjected to the same earthquake intensity levels.

CHAPTER V

RESULTS AND DISCUSSIONS

Site characterization

Carig Sur barangay officials claim a total of 708 households in the area on top of the government structures housing the different offices in the region. In the actual survey, the number of households, however, was 798. This discrepancy can be explained by the fact that during the survey, residential buildings (104) near the university might not have been accounted for and which would have not been part of their present records.

Carig Sur is also one of the biggest barangays in the city. Majority of this, however, are agricultural fields or are partly hilly where building structures are yet to be erected. Among the current structures found include 34 used by other government agencies and the regional hospital and 44 from schools.

Centro 6, on the other hand, forms part of the commercial district of Tuguegarao City. It also has a school, a hospital, a number of private clinics, hotels, fast food centers, and a mall. Other sections are used purely for residential purposes.

Centro 10 has a mosque and a cathedral, a hotel, a park and the rest are residential areas. Makeshift structures, however, are common in the area.

Development of exposure database

A total of 1,335 buildings were surveyed from the three barangays of which 83 are government-owned. The bulk of these buildings are located in Carig Sur at 868 (65%) while the least number come from Centro 6 at 88 (6.5%).

Three different exposure databases were developed separately for each of the barangays. The maps are developed for easy interpretation and would be of great help to quick response team/s to areas affected. The extent of damages and affected people can also be easily deduced from the maps.

Delineation of land use and building statistics

Actual landuse for each segment of the barangays were produced out of the data gathered. Prescribed landuse categories and color codes were adapted for uniformity of interpretation. Summary of the building categories according to use can be found in Appendix 4 (Table A2). Figures 12, 13, & 14 below show the actual landuse for barangays Carig Sur, Centro 6 and Centro 10, respectively.

26

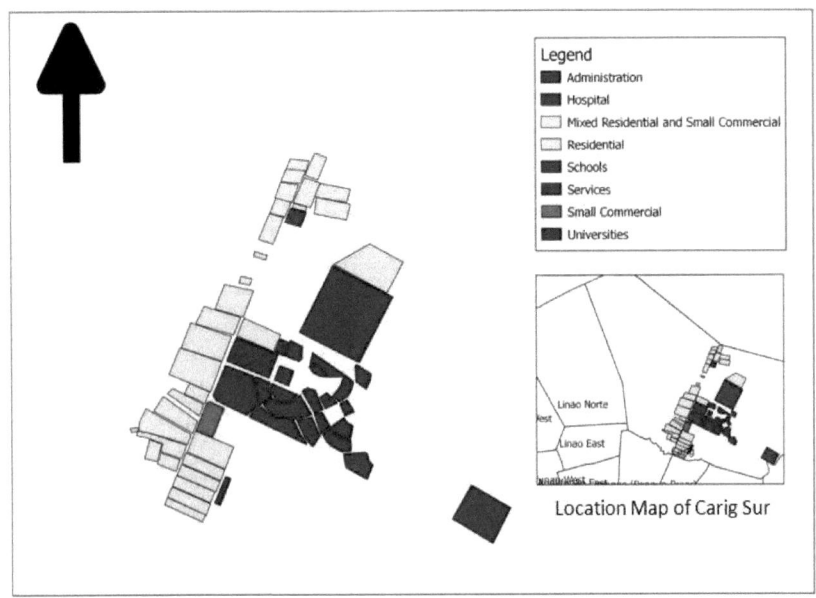

Fig. 12. Actual landuse of Carig Sur. Not shown are areas for agriculture or parks and open spaces.

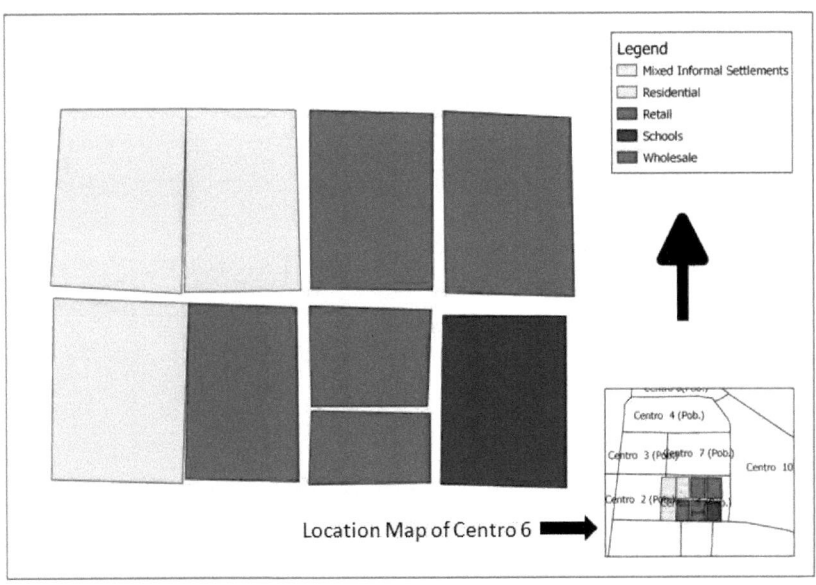

Fig. 13. Actual landuse of Centro 6.

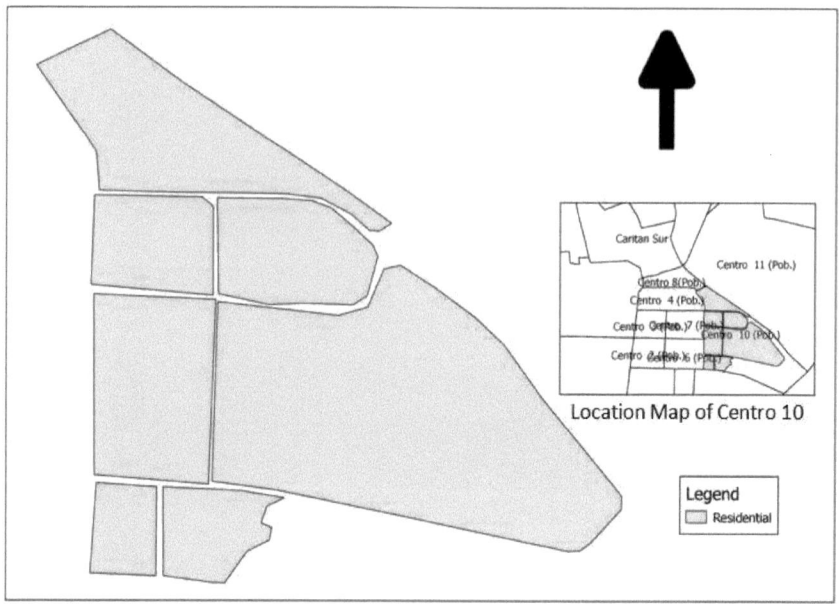

Fig. 14. Actual landuse of Centro 10.

While these maps show the generalized use in each block or segment of the barangay, the actual distribution of what these are made of are shown in the succeeding figures.

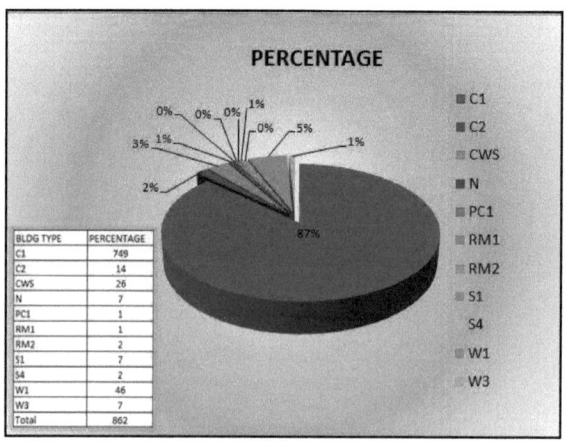

Fig. 15. Building type distribution in Carig Sur.

28

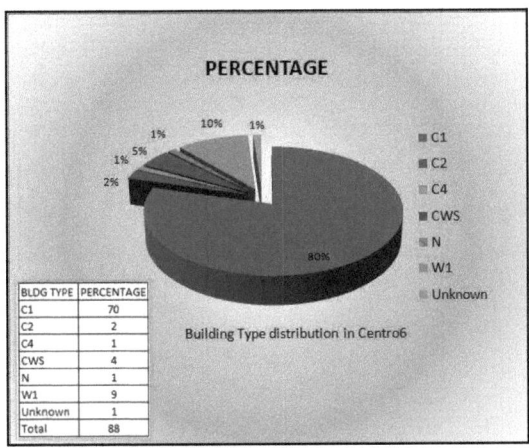

BLDG TYPE	PERCENTAGE
C1	70
C2	2
C4	1
CWS	4
N	1
W1	9
Unknown	1
Total	88

Fig. 16. Building type distribution in Centro 6.

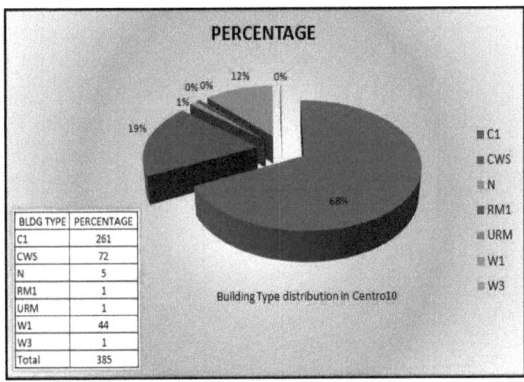

BLDG TYPE	PERCENTAGE
C1	261
CWS	72
N	5
RM1	1
URM	1
W1	44
W3	1
Total	385

Fig. 17. Building type distribution in Centro 10.

Notably, the C1 (Reinforced Concrete Moment Frames) type of buildings are dominant in all the pilot sites. In Carig Sur (Fig. 15) alone, this represents 87% of the buildings followed by W1 (Wood, Light Frame) representing a low 5% of the total structures. Similarly, Centro 6 is comprised of 80% C1 buildings and again followed by W1 at 10% (Fig. 16). While C1 still tops the types of buildings in Centro 10 at 68%, this, however, is followed by CWS buildings (19%). CWS type is a hybrid characterized by a combination of reinforced concrete moment frames (at the lower floor) and wood or light metal (at the second floor).

Distribution of building type per barangay:

As described in Figs. 15, 16, & 17, most of the buildings in the pilot sites are of the C1 type representing 81% (1080/1335). These can, however, be further subdivided as C1L (low) if it is up to 2 storeys high; C1M (medium) from 3-7 storeys; and C1H (high) from 8-15 storeys. Running next is W1 at 7.4% and CWS at 2.4%.

29

C1 buildings can rise from (1) storey to 15 storeys high. While Figs. 15-17 show actual count of individual buildings, it still could not give us a complete view of the amount of damages if ever it would occur. Depending on the magnitude of an earthquake, the degree of damage that can be expected varies as a function of the distance from the epicenter and the fault. To estimate the cost of damages, we use the total floor area as a benchmark and the average cost required to re-construct a certain type of building.

Figs. 18-20 show us a glimpse of the possible damages and probable locations.

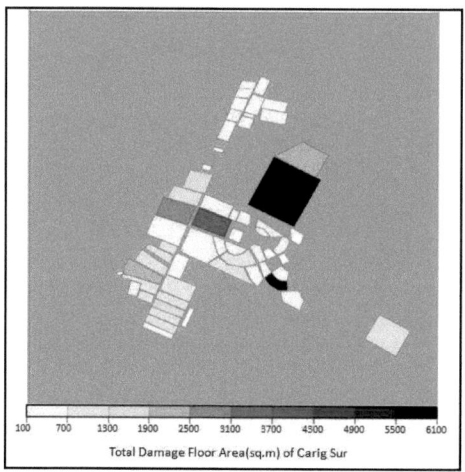

Fig. 18. Floor damage forecast and site incidence in Carig Sur.

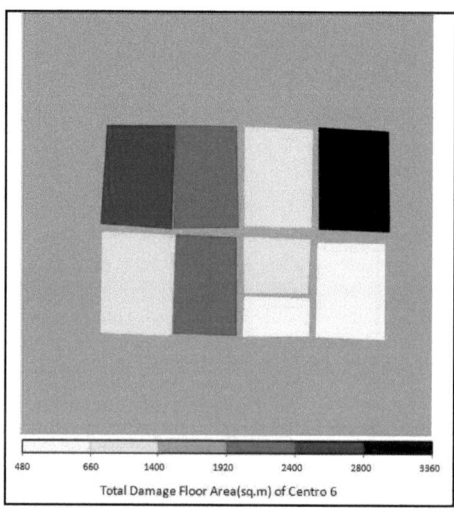

Fig. 19. Floor damage forecast and site incidence in Centro 6.

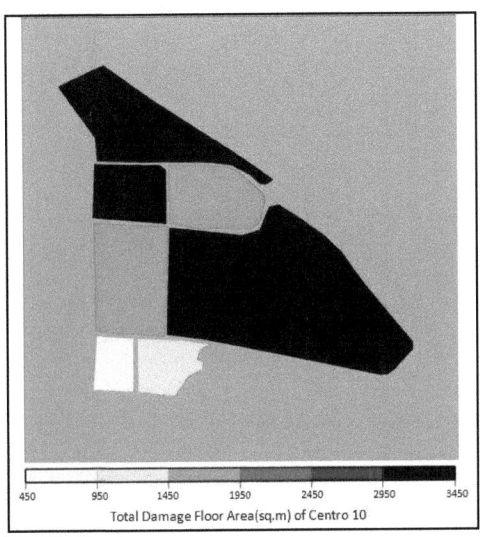

Fig. 20. Floor damage forecast and site incidence in Centro 10.

With these damages, the average cost can be applied to arrive at how much would it cost to replace the damaged structures. For example, the cost of constructing a C1 versus a CWS of the same floor area differs a lot. Experienced builders can provide us average values for different types of structures.

The figures below give us the expected replacement costs for the projected damages as given previously. (Note: The cost of construction is proportional to the damaged area.)

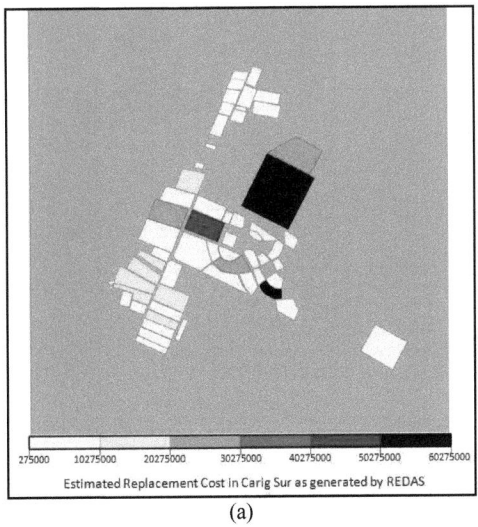

(a)

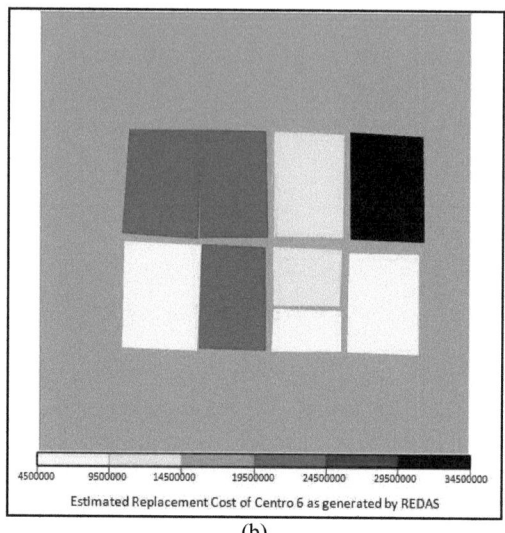

4500000   9500000   14500000   19500000   24500000   29500000   34500000

Estimated Replacement Cost of Centro 6 as generated by REDAS

(b)

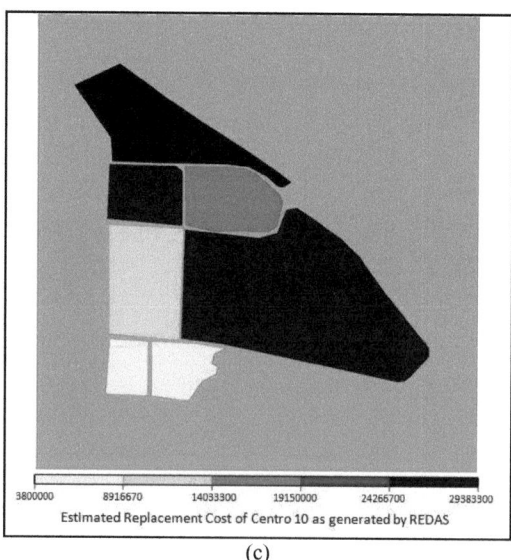

3800000   8916670   14033300   19150000   24266700   29383300

Estimated Replacement Cost of Centro 10 as generated by REDAS

(c)

Fig. 21a, b, c. Corresponding costs to replace the estimated damages (in the three barangays) after an earthquake.

Era of construction:

Aside from the building type as an important input parameter in determining the damage probability, the year of construction is also to be considered. Recall that prior to 1972 era, no

32

specific guidelines have been adopted by structural engineers in the Philippines to address earthquake effects on building structures. In 1977 though, the National Building Code of the Philippines (NBCP) through PD 1096 has come into existence. Thereon, several editions of the code have continuously evolved to consider problems not fully addressed in its current issues.

To address concerns not properly covered in the NBCP, and as an off-shoot of the July 16, 1990 earthquake in Luzon, new provisions were included in the National Structural Code of the Philippines (NSCP) after 1992. To date, the latest version was published in 2012.

Table 5. Distribution of period of construction of the buildings surveyed in the three barangays.

Era of construction	Pre-1972	1972-1992	Post 1992	Total
Carig Sur	4	81	777	862
Centro 6	1	21	66	88
Centro 10	9	58	318	385
Total	14	160	1161	**1335**

In general, 87% of the buildings were constructed after 1992. Assuming full compliance of the structural provisions by the NSCP, less damages would be expected. Fig. 18, however, reveals something that is very alarming. The big dark rectangular block is exactly where Cagayan State University at Carig is located! With 34 individual structures inside the campus, only six were built after 1992. Others existed in the late 70's when CSU was founded. To gain an insight on why this much of expected damage, let us compare both C1 buildings but were constructed at different era.

Fig. 22 shows us the fragility curves generated for a C1L building built between 1972-1992 (mid-era). Coincidentally, another C1L built after 1992 reveals the same damage probability when subjected to a magnitude 7.0 earthquake. Though the structures are built on different periods, the likelihood that they will be damaged are the same, hence the common dark shaded area (Fig. 18) over the block.

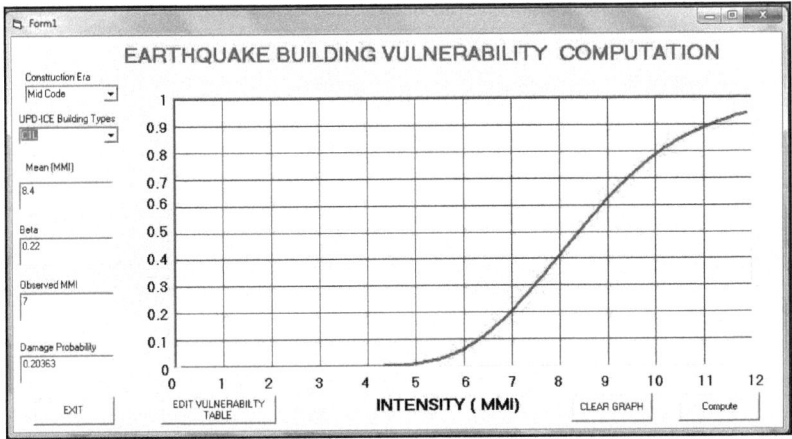

Fig. 22. Fragility curve for C1L building built between 1972-1992 subjected to a magnitude 7.0 earthquake (Damage probability ≈ 20%).

Another second look should be conducted at the Cagayan Valley Medical Center (CVMC) area as it ranks next to CSU in terms of the expected damages. In cases of catastrophes like earthquakes, the hospitals act as a point of convergence for rescue operations. Hence, the soundness of the building to withstand the same should be a priority. Construction of new and state-of-the-art buildings are now on-going in the medical center as part of their health services expansion program.

In contrast, most of the new government structures in the area are coded light – an indication that these could withstand the same magnitude of earthquake that would damage most of the buildings in the university. Worst, though, is the Regional office of the Department of Environment & Natural Resources (DENR) as it gains the top spot with the darkest shade. DENR Region 02 office is a 4-storey building.

Another alarming observation is at Centro 6 where the Paseo Reale and Tuguegarao People's General Hospital (TPGH) are located. From Fig. 19, this block has the highest total floor area to be affected. This is because these buildings are multi-storey compared to the rest within the vicinity. Like the case of CVMC, objective evaluation of the current structures (Paseo Reale & TPGH) must be given priority as these are public places and center of health services, respectively. It is also good to note that the area where Tuguegarao East Central School is located will only have minimal damages.

The greatest damaged areas in Carig Sur and Centro 6 approximately range from 15-25% of the buildings surveyed. In Centro 10, more than half of the structures (Fig. 20) expect the greatest damages. Only about less than 5% will suffer less damages (Rizal St. corner Arellano St.) including the present location of the Provincial jail.

Surprisingly, there is no difference between the damage probabilities generated from the different structural types but constructed at different periods. This might be due to the fact that nowhere in the National Building Code of the Philippines (2005) covers concerns about compliance to earthquake requirements. In lieu thereof, the National Structural Code of the Philippines (NSCP) is used as reference.

Earthquake risk and loss estimation

With this current scenario, the following estimates can be deduced from the data gathered. Assuming an intensity 7 earthquake will be observed in the area, the following losses due to damages are estimated. (Note: Intensity is used here rather than magnitude because historic records show that there has been no earthquake event recorded with epicenter at Tuguegarao City. The tremors felt are results from earthquakes emanating from distant epicenters.)

The values were obtained by using the average cost of construction per type of building as follows:

Table 6. Cost per unit area used in forecasting damages due to earthquake.

Type of Building*	Average cost of construction per square meter (P)**
C1	13,000
CWS	11,000
W1	10,000

*These types (UP-ICE) are used being the dominant building types in the areas covered.
** The values are based from the experience of a structural engineer and land developer .

Table 7. Estimated cost of damages in Carig Sur

Bldg type	#	Floor area (m²)	Damage probability	Damaged floor (in m²)	Estimated cost/m² (P)			Total cost (P)
					13k	11k	10k	
C1	749	94211.6	0.2015	18,984	246792000			246792000
CWS	26	3064.7	0.0234	72		792000		792000
W1	46	3375	0.2043	690			6900000	6900000
				19,746				254484000

Table 8. Estimated cost of damages in Centro 6

Bldg type	#	Floor area (m²)	Damage probability	Damaged floor (in m²)	Estimated cost/m² (P)			Total cost (P)
					13k	11k	10k	
C1	70	29562.4	0.2015	5,957	77441000			77441000
CWS	4	592	0.0234	14		154000		154000
W1	9	1622	0.2043	331			3310000	3310000
				6302				80905000

Table 9. Estimated cost of damages in Centro 10

Bldg type	#	Floor area (m²)	Damage probability	Damaged floor (in m²)	Estimated cost/m² (P)			Total cost (P)
					13k	11k	10k	
C1	70	261	0.2015	4,865	63245000			63245000
CWS	4	72	0.0234	147		1617000		1617000
W1	9	44	0.2043	502			5020000	5020000
				5,514				69882000

To complete the analysis, we shall consider the number of people directly affected if this event will happen. Similarly, we take 20% (from damage probability of the majority of the buildings) of the population as those that will directly bear the consequences of destruction. Also, the number of occupants in the surveyed structures was taken as a lower to higher range (e.g. 1-5, 6-10, etc). In some cases, no occupants were present in the dwellings during the conduct of the survey.

The projected estimates on the number of people directly affected were based on night earthquake event where residents are supposed to be at home. Non-residents like students, employers/employees, and other private citizens that are usually in the city during the day are not considered.

Table 10. Projected number of directly affected people during an earthquake in Carig Sur.

Bldg Type	Estimated Occupants		Estimated directly affected occupants	
	Lower	Higher	Lower	Higher
C1	6544	14020	1309	2804
CWS	110	270	22	54
W1	221	530	44	106
			1375	2964

Table 11. Projected number of directly affected people during an earthquake in Centro 6.

Bldg Type	Estimated Occupants		Estimated directly affected occupants	
	Lower	Higher	Lower	Higher
C1	1792	5640	358	1128
CWS	19	35	4	7
W1	53	115	11	23
			373	1158

Table 12. Projected number of directly affected people during an earthquake in Centro 10.

Bldg Type	Estimated Occupants		Estimated directly affected occupants	
	Lower	Higher	Lower	Higher
C1	1456	3355	291	671
CWS	361	785	72	157
W1	174	3758	35	752
			398	1580

In the foregoing estimates, an intensity 7 earthquake was assumed. This gives us a comparative view of how would Tuguegarao City be if it were like the case of Bohol. Intensity 7 was used regardless of the exact location of an earthquake with an epicenter outside Tuguegarao City. The farther the epicenter from the area under study, the lesser is the intensity felt in the locality. The nearest fault identified in the province is the one located in the municipality of Baggao, Cagayan in the Sierra Madre mountain range.

C1, CWS, and W1 types of buildings were used in the simulation as these represent majority of the building types. The different damage probabilities were generated from the fragility curves as formulated from the study conducted by the University of the Philippines- Institute of Civil Engineering.

In Carig Sur, this will likely cost P255 M affecting between 1400 to 3000 people; Centro 6 will cost about P81 M and affecting 400 – 1200 and will also cost P 70 M to about 1000 people of Centro 10. This will likely happen, though, once in 200 years!

Generalized Forecasts

The magnitude 7.2 earthquake (with intensity 7 effect) considered above is alarming. With a very low probability of occurrence of 0.5%, this event never happened in Tuguegarao City. To ease concerns for the remote eventuality, a general forecast for the lower intensities are hereby considered for the top three types of buildings encountered.

Fig. 23 shows the damage probabilities as generated by the UP-ICE fragility curves for intensities 4 – 8 for C1, CWS, and W1 types of buildings. As depicted in the graph, the CWS buildings are the most prone to damages while C1 are the least affected. A 4.0 earthquake though will unlikely result to significant damages. The same curve will be used in the three barangays to simulate the amount of damages and the number of people directly affected in each. It will be noted that the amount of damages and number of people affected also follow a logarithmic function as given in the figures.

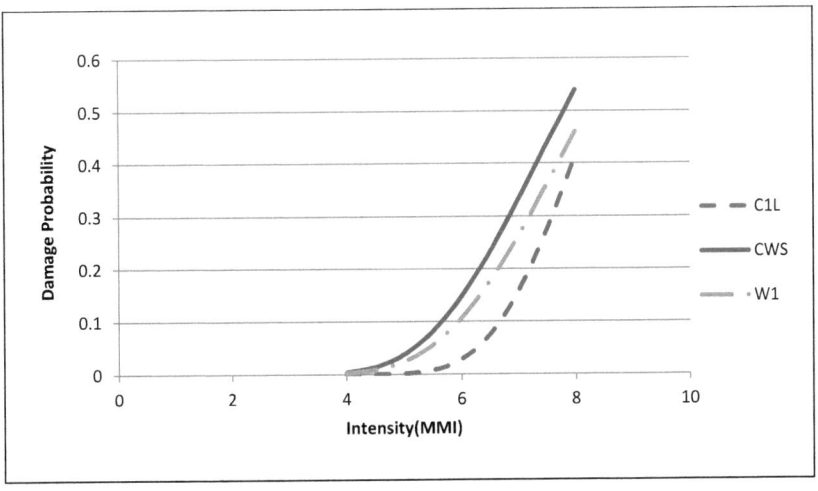

Fig. 23. Generalized damage probabilities for different types of buildings subjected to different intensities of earthquake.

In Carig Sur, significant damages are expected between intensities 6-8 with replacement cost ranging from 43 to 540 M and affecting about 360 to 4500 (Figs 24 & 25)

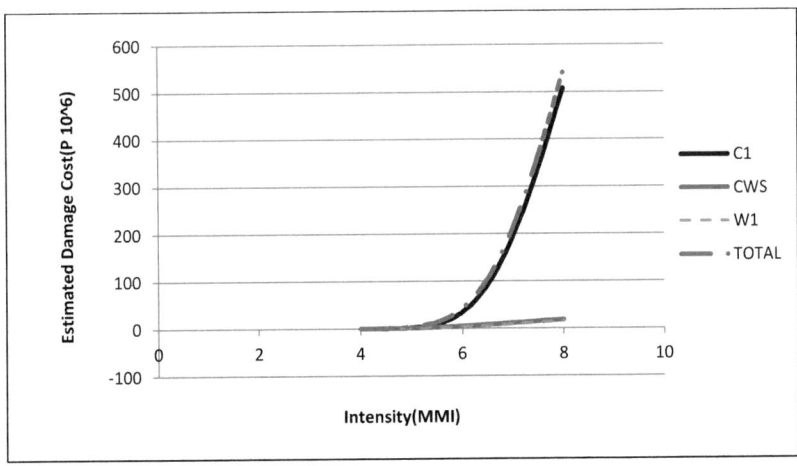

Fig. 24. Estimated replacement cost in Carig Sur for different intensities of earthquake.

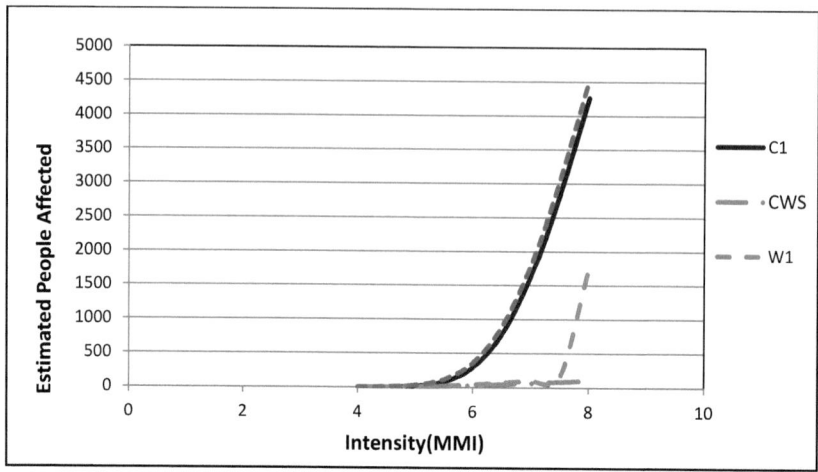

Fig. 25. Estimated number of people directly affected for different intensities of earthquake in Carig Sur.

Similarly, Figs. 26-29 give the replacement cost of damages and people affected in Centro 6 and Centro 10. Table 13 gives the summary of estimated replacement cost of damages and affected people for the three barangays. It should be noted that as the intensity of earthquake increases, its probability of occurrence decreases. However, higher damages would occur from stronger quakes! C1 buildings approximate the total costs generated for Carig Sur and Centro 6 as these represent 81% of the total buildings surveyed.

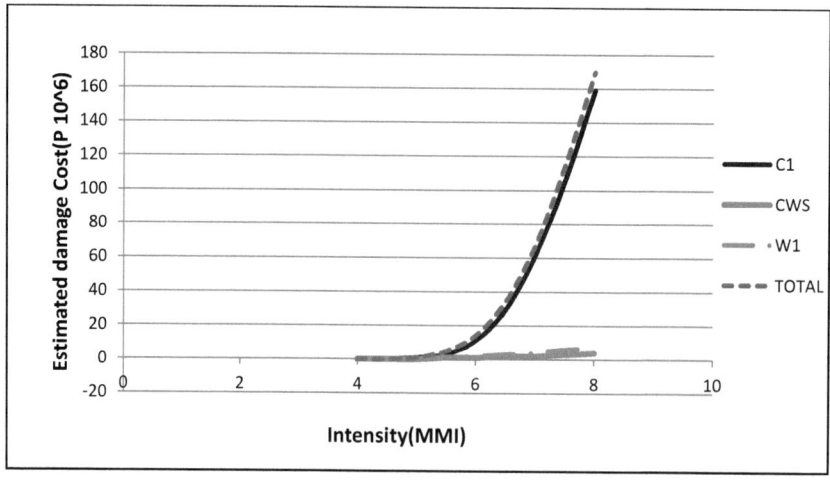

Fig. 26. Estimated replacement cost in Centro 6 for different intensities of earthquake.

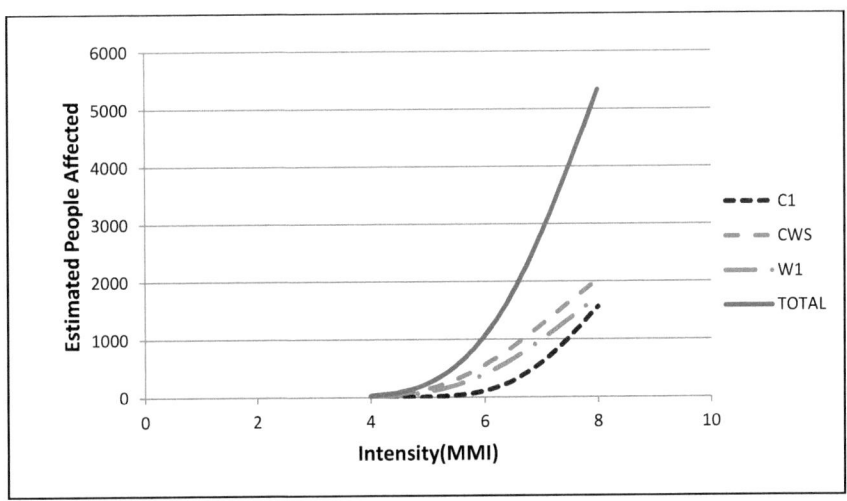

Fig. 27. Estimated number of people directly affected for different intensities of earthquake in Centro 6.

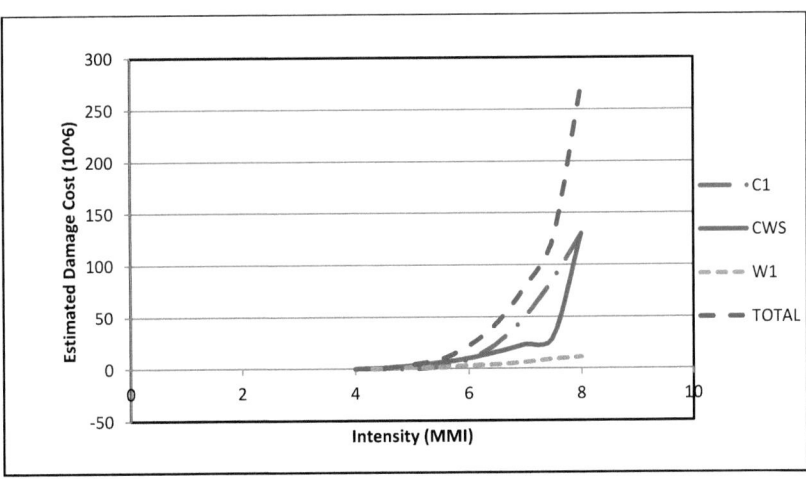

Fig. 28. Estimated replacement cost in Centro 10 for different intensities of earthquake.

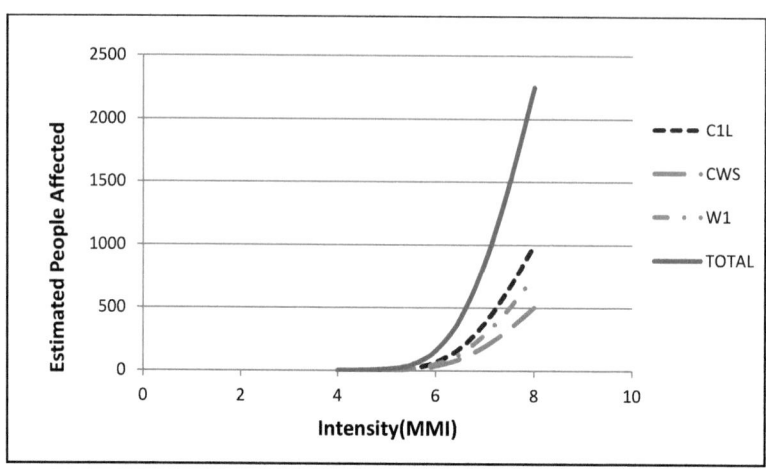

Fig. 29. Estimated number of people directly affected for different intensities of earthquake in Centro 10.

Table 13. Summary of estimated effects of earthquake with intensity ranging from 6-8 in three different barangays of Tuguegarao City.

Barangay	Estimated replacement costs (P 10^6)		Estimated people affected	
	Lower	Upper	Lower	Upper
Carig Sur	43	541	358	4536
Centro 6	14	170	1058	5330
Centro 10	22	271	158	2250

The figures above should help the local officials in coordination with Disaster Risk Reduction Management Officers (DRRMO) to formulate and plan necessary measures to curb this eventuality. Education of the people through proper information drive accompanied by simulation drills would help a lot.

Upgraded capabilities of REDAS

The most recent version of the software has been equipped with capabilities to come up with building damage and loss estimates. It considers physical damage and equivalent economic loss and can generate certain degrees of casualties ranging from those incurring minor injuries to those that can be fatally affected. The results can be in table form or in shape files expressed in plot loss maps.

Using the same survey data as collected in the study and available Philippine NSO files, the following forecasts were obtained by using the "*paintbrushing*" technique. This results from extrapolation of the localized estimates in the three pilot barangays for the whole City of Tuguegarao and the province of Cagayan. In the foregoing section, magnitude 8.0 earthquake was used being the greatest ever recorded event that occurred in the region (November 30, 1619).

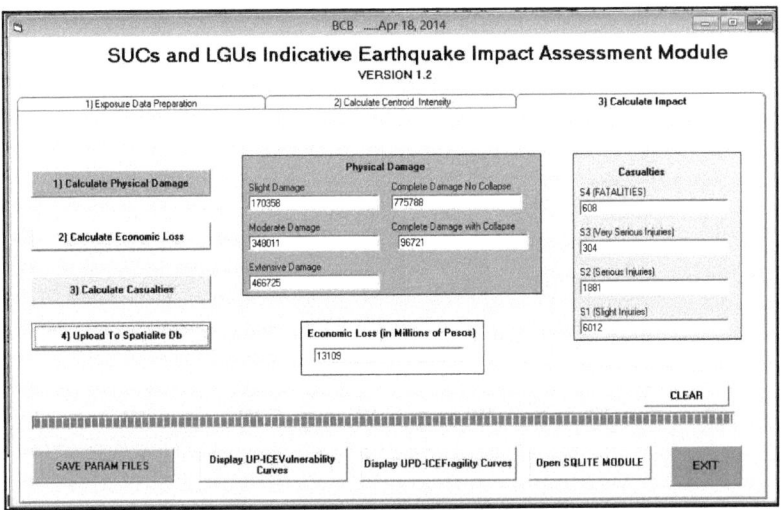

Fig. 30. Forecasts generated from actual survey data for a magnitude 8.0 earthquake in Tuguegarao City, Cagayan Province, Philippines.

The earlier version 1.2 of the Earthquake Assessment Module, estimates the localized physical damages expressed in terms of damaged floor area are as follows:

Slight damage -- 170,358 m²
Moderate damage -- 348,011 m²
Extensive damage --- 466, 725 m²
Complete damage with no collapse ------------------- 775,788 m²
Complete damage with collapse ---------------------- 96,721 m²

This corresponds to an economic loss of about 13 billion pesos (USD 300 M)

The same earthquake event would likely result to the following casualties:

Fatalities -- 608
Very serious injuries ------------------------------------ 304
Serious injuries --- 1,881
Slight injuries --- 6,012

While the conduct of actual surveys for the different areas are considered tedious and time-consuming, it is, however, essential part of the study. To lessen the burden of getting these first-hand data, an equally dependable alternative is to utilize existing data from the NSO. The NSO, formerly known as Bureau of Census and Statistics is the Philippine government's major statistical agency responsible in collecting, compiling, classifying, producing, publishing, and disseminating general-purpose statistics (https://en.wikipedia.org/wiki/Philippine Statistics Authority/August 18, 2015).

Similarly, when using the NSO data, the estimates below are generated:

41

Physical Damages:

Slight damage -- 166,226 m^2
Moderate damage ------------------------------------- 329,655 m^2
Extensive damage ------------------------------------ 321,523 m^2
Complete damage with no collapse ------------------- 929,898 m^2
Complete damage with collapse ---------------------- 66,478 m^2

Economic loss:

12.3 billion pesos (USD 280 M)

Casualties:

Fatalities -- 900
Very serious injuries ------------------------------------ 452
Serious injuries --- 3,755
Slight injuries --- 13,755

The discrepancies in the values generated from the two data sources can be explained by the more generality of the data as obtained from NSO. It, however, gives an easier assessment of the effects of the tremors in a larger scale where immediate and more detailed survey activity is impossible especially when conducting a rapid assessment of the damages. This gives proper authorities the ability to reasonably implement appropriate measures in the conduct of relief and rescue operations.

A more general forecast can also be generated for the whole province of Cagayan which is comprised of 29 municipalities. Using the same data obtained from actual survey and from the NSO, a similar approach can be done and the distribution over the entire area can be viewed from the shapefiles. This gives a brief overview of the distribution and extent of damages and casualties in the different areas.

For example, while specific values are given in the earthquake assessment module, a map generalizing the distribution of the damages can likewise be drawn. Fig. 31 shows the computed damages and Figs. 32a to 32c are the corresponding maps of the physical damages, economic loss and fatalities, respectively, in the different municipalities in Cagayan.

The damages are summarized as follows:

Physical damages:

Slight damage -- 896,264 m^2
Moderate damage ------------------------------------- 1,710,714 m^2
Extensive damage ------------------------------------ 2,219,596 m^2
Complete damage with no collapse ------------------- 3,858,968 m^2
Complete damage with collapse ---------------------- 481,439 m^2

Economic loss:

63.4 billion pesos (USD 1.4 B)

Casualties:

Fatalities -- 4,685
Very serious injuries ------------------------------------ 2,230
Serious injuries --- 14,129
Slight injuries --- 46,202

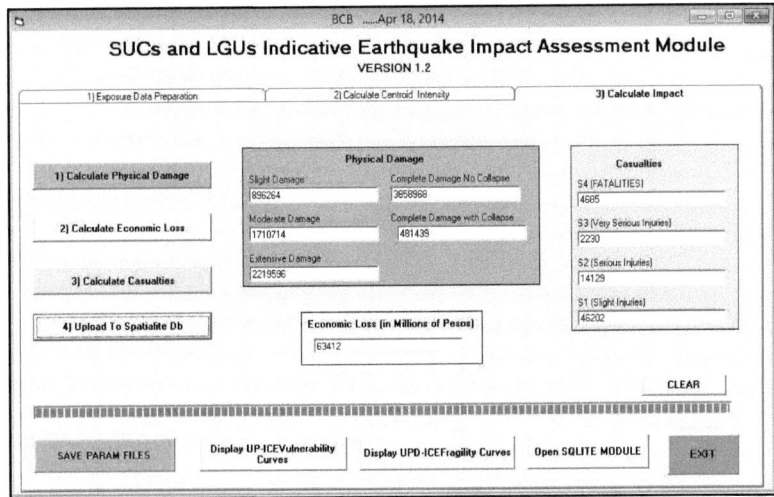

Fig. 31. Forecasts generated from actual survey data for a magnitude 8.0 earthquake in the entire Cagayan Province, Philippines.

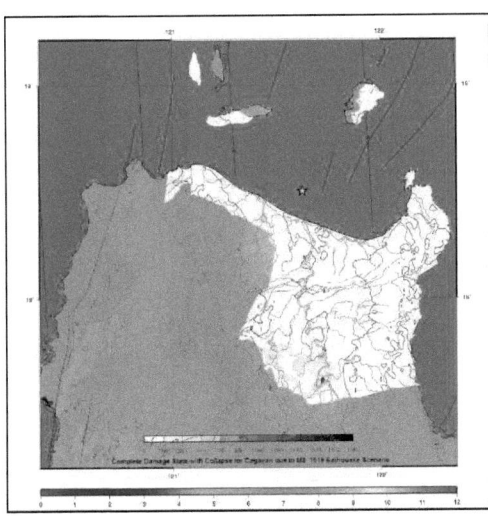

Fig. 32a. Distribution and extent of damages in the province of Cagayan.

43

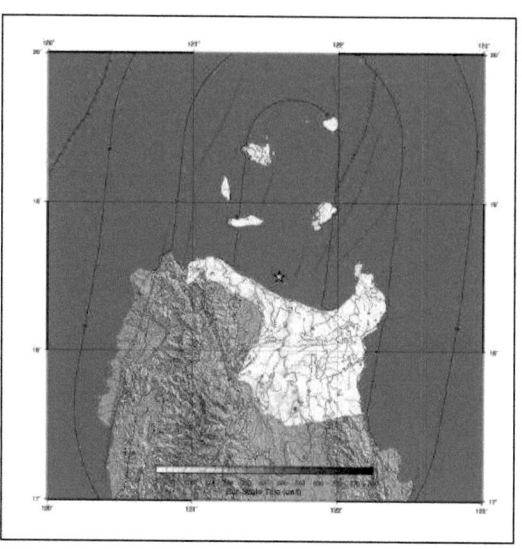

Fig. 32b. Economic loss due to magnitude 8.0 earthquake in the province of Cagayan.

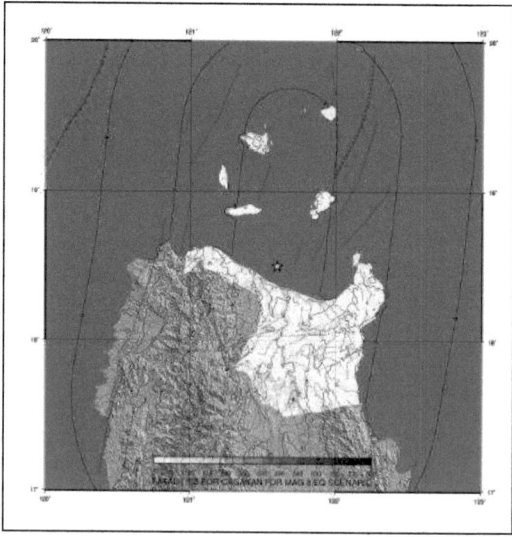

Fig. 32c. Distribution and extent of casualties in the province of Cagayan.

44

On the other hand, the NSO data yields following damages (Table 10) and casualties (Table 11) resulting to an economic loss of approximately equal to P53.2 billion (USD 1.2 M):

Table 14. Tabular estimates of the physical damages for the whole province of Cagayan using NSO data. (Note the increased capabilities of version 1.4 of the Earthquake Assessment Module as compared to the previous version wherein the total number of buildings affected are also hereby given.)

Physical damages	Total floor area (m²)	No. of buildings affected
Slight damage	940,455	22,901
Moderate damage	1,582,271	37,338
Extensive damage	1,763,485	41,507
Complete damage with no collapse	4,586,592	111,246
Complete damage with collapse	305,295	7,237

Table 15. Estimated casualties from magnitude 8.0 earthquake in the province of Cagayan using NSO data.

Fatalities	2,611
Life threatening	1,161
Non-life threatening	11,989
Slight injuries	45,900

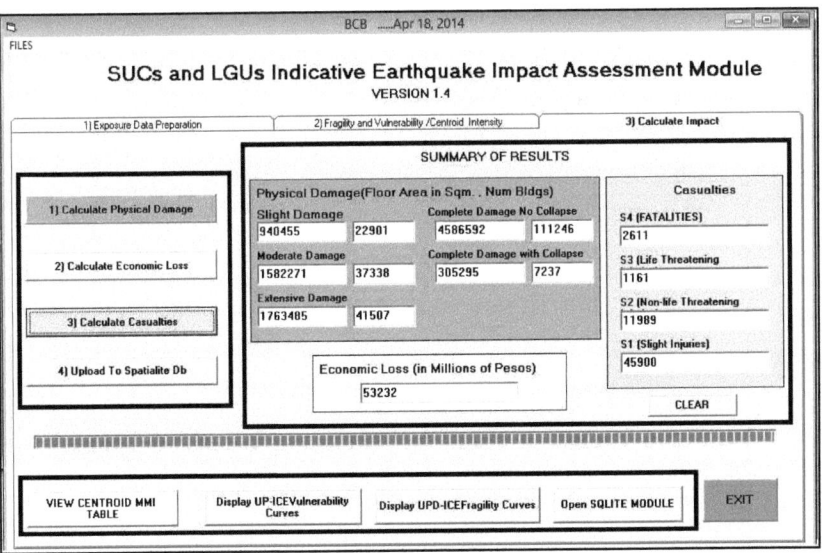

Fig. 33. Forecasts generated from NSO survey data for a magnitude 8.0 earthquake in the entire Cagayan Province, Philippines using version 1.4 of the SUC's and LGU's Indicative Earthquake Assessment Module.

Since the earlier versions of REDAS, new capabilities have been developed that tremendously facilitate the work of planners and administrators in coming up with appropriate actions and decisions in areas affected by related disasters. In fact, the programmers and contributors are closely coordinating with officials of the Philippine Atmospheric, Geophysical and Astronomical Services Administration (PAGASA) in working out the inclusion of rapid assessment of the effects of floods and typhoons (high winds) in affected areas.

PAGASA is a Philippine national institution dedicated to provide flood and typhoon warnings, public weather forecasts and advisories, meteorological, astronomical, climatological, and other specialized information and services primarily for the protection of life and property and in support of economic, productivity and sustainable development.

Legislative measures towards risk reduction

The above scenario set to be experienced by the pilot area has been pegged at the worst possible level of conditions. This should form bases of certain legislations to be enforced with strictest monitoring to include:

1. Proper implementation and adaption of sound engineering principles and practices to address the vulnerability of structures in the area;
2. Identification in the land-use plans areas traversed by fault lines highlighting the buffer zones to regulate and control erection of utilities that might endanger lives;
3. Operationalize a regular earthquake drill and information drive in each locality and identifying specific evacuation plans during actual events;
4. Mobilize a core group composed of personnel with specialized trainings to be involved in emergency and rescue operations; and
5. Allocation of funds for the purchase of lifeline utilities and supplies that can be readily available when they are needed.

A network to instill cooperation and awareness among local government units (LGUs) must also be organized so that communication and response units can be easily mobilized as the need arises. REDAS likewise is equipped with a module called Earthquake and Tsunami Alerting Module (ETAM) which can be a source of reliable information of the different earthquake events indicating thereat the magnitude and location within near-real time fashion. This requires, however, good internet connections to avail of these services.

Limitations of the Study

The damage costs generated were based on building costs only and do not include costs from other facilities and/or equipment that might have been damaged inside the buildings at the time of the quake.

No simulations were done on the incidence of tsunami as Tuguegarao City is an inland area and has no coastal areas that will be directly affected. Likewise, the occurrence of landslides and liquefaction have not been studied due to limitations on the scope of the study. REDAS, however, is equipped with these capabilities.

CHAPTER VI

CONCLUSION

Eighty-one percent of the buildings surveyed in Tuguegarao City are made up of reinforced concrete moment frames (C1) followed by W1 (7.4%) and CWS (2.4%) while 87% were built after 1992. The survey was conducted in barangays Carig Sur, Centro 6 and Centro 10.

Using the majority of the building types as a basis, a 7.2 earthquake that will hit Tuguegarao City would cost about P 255M affecting 1400-3000 people in Carig Sur; P 81M affecting 400-1200 in Centro 6; and P 70M affecting about 1000 people in Centro 10. Extrapolation of these values for the entire City reveals that this costs about P13 B in economic loss resulting to 6,012 slight injuries; 1,881 serious injuries; 304 very serious injuries; and 608 fatalities. The entire province of Cagayan will expect economic loss of P 63.4 B and projected 46,202 slight injuries; 14,129 serious injuries; 2,230 very serious injuries; and 4,685 fatalities. These values are based on impact estimation and ground-shaking simulations only excluding the effects of possible landslides, liquefaction, and/or tsunami. Other losses due to non-structural damages are not considered in the study.

LITERATURE CITED

Foz, Vicente B. editor/publisher. *The National Building Code of the Philippines* (with its revised implementing rules & regulations). 2007

Bautista, Ma. Leonila. Presentor. REDAS as a risk assessment tool. Cagayan province REDAS training. December 3-8, 2014

Bautista, Ma. Leonila. Presentor. Earthquake risk assessment steps. Cagayan province REDAS training. December 3-8, 2014

Ali, Aamir. *Earthquake Safety Measures*. March 24, 2008. http://www.merinews.com/article/earthquake-safety-measures/131229.shtml#sthash.IyzYa2gD.dpuf/10/21/2013

Kamiri, H, M. Skandarski, R. P. Sivashanmugham and F. Feber. *Vulnerability to Earthquake*. Paper presented at the United Nations University – Institute for Environment and Human Security/April 2010/ UN Campus, Bonn

Lanuza, Angelito G. *Case Study for Land Use Planning using REDAS: Vulnerability of Gabaldon, N.E. to Earthquake Hazards*. PHIVOLCS. 2012

Local Government Code of the Philippines

Association of Structural Engineers of the Philippines. National Structural Code of the Philippines. Vol. 1. Buildings, Towers & other Structures. 6th ed. 2012

Federal Emergency Management Agency (FEMA). *Reducing the risks of nonstructural earthquake damage - a practical guide, fourth edition*. USA/2011. 755 p.

ISO/IEC. Risk Management-Vocabulary-Guidelines for Use in Standards. ISO/IEC Guide 73. 2002

Philippine Daily Inquirer, June 8, 2013 issue

Philippine Institute of Volcanology and Seismology- Department of Science & Technology

Risk Management Solutions, Inc., 2009.

LIVESCIENCE video on "Earthquake: What does magnitude mean?"

REDAS Manual

Facebook.com

http://www.dotregion2.com.ph/d2/index.php?option=com_content&view=article&id=71&Itemid=83

http://www.abs-cbnnews.com/nation/metro-manila/10/17/13/magnitude-72-quake-metro-manila-will-kill-37000

http://earthquake.usgs.gov/learn/topics/mag_vs_int.php/10-22-2013
http://en.wikipedia.org/wiki/Richter_magnitude_scale

http://en.wikipedia.org/wiki/Earthquake/10-23-2013

http://www.sunstar.com.ph/ manila/61-magnitude-quake-rattles-tuguegarao

https://en.wikipedia.org/wiki/April_2015_Nepal_earthquake/August 18, 2015

https://en.wikipedia.org/wiki/May_2015_Nepal_earthquake/August 18, 2015

https://en.wikipedia.org/wiki/Philippine_Statistics_Authority/August 18, 2015

APPENDIX

Appendix 1:

Structured questionnaire used for building survey

1. Name of Owner_____
2. Coordinates of Building   Longitude:_____
   Latitude_____
3. Location
   Municipality_____ Barangay_____Purok No._____Street No._____ St.
Name_____
4. **_Bldg. Use 1_**

Use 1	Use 1 Percent	Use 1 People
1 - Industrial	1 - Unknown	1 - None
2 - Residential;	2 - 0%	2 - 1 to 5
3 - Government	3 - 10%	3 - 6 to 10
4 - Hospital	4 - 20%	4 - 11 to 20
5 - Office	5 - 30%	5 - 21 to 50
6 - Agriculture	6 - 40%	6 - 51 to 100
7 - Other	7 - 50%	7 - 101 to 500
8 - Unknown	8 - 60%	8 - 501 to 1000
	9 - 70%	9 - 1001 to 5000
	10 - 80%	10 - > 5000
	11 - 90%	11 - Unknown
	12 - 100%	

Bldg Use 2

Use 1	Use 1 Percent	Use 1 People
1 - Industrial	1 - Unknown	1 - None
2 - Residential;	2 - 0%	2 - 1 to 5
3 - Government	3 - 10%	3 - 6 to 10
4 - Hospital	4 - 20%	4 - 11 to 20
5 - Office	5 - 30%	5 - 21 to 50
6 - Agriculture	6 - 40%	6 - 51 to 100
7 - Other	7 - 50%	7 - 101 to 500
8 - Unknown	8 - 60%	8 - 501 to 1000
	9 - 70%	9 - 1001 to 5000
	10 - 80%	10 - > 5000
	11 - 90%	11 - Unknown
	12 - 100%	

Bldg Use 3

Use 1	Use 1 Percent	Use 1 People
1 - Industrial	1 - Unknown	1 - None
2 - Residential;	2 - 0%	2 - 1 to 5
3 - Government	3 - 10%	3 - 6 to 10
4 - Hospital	4 - 20%	4 - 11 to 20
5 - Office	5 - 30%	5 - 21 to 50
6 - Agriculture	6 - 40%	6 - 51 to 100
7 - Other	7 - 50%	7 - 101 to 500

PHOTOGRAPHS (file name)

1._____
2._____
3._____
4._____

5. Building Structure

Year Built (Range)	Bldg. Type	Primary Vertical Plan Shape	Secondary Vertical Plan Shape	Horizontal Plan Shape
	1 - Apartment House	1 - Multiple Towers	1 - Split levels 2 - Non-distribution of mass	1 - L shaped
(1) - Pre-1972	2 - Hotel 3 - Boarding House	2 - Split levels 3 - Non-distribution of Mass	3 - Heavy ornament	2 - T Shaped 3 - Hollow
(2) - 1972-1992	4 - Lodging House 5 - Accessory Bldg.	4 - Heavy ornament 5 - Long cantilever	4 - Long Cantilever 5 - Tall tower or chimney	4 - Triangular 5 - Circular
(3) – Post 1992	6 - Office Bldg	6 - Tall tower or chimney	6 - Soft Storey 7 - Large/irregular opening in walls	6 - Polygonal 7 - U shaped
Year Built (Exact): _____	7 - Theater 8 - Warehouse	7 - Soft Storey 8 - Large/irregular opening in walls	8 - Transfer structures	8 - X cranked 9 - Rectangular
Width (m):_____ Depth(m):_____	9 - Residential	9 - Transfer Structures 10 - Interruption of beams		
No. of Storeys:_____		11 - Openings in Floors 12 - Mixed Structural systems 13 - Building on hillside		

Overall Condition	Seismic Separation (Left)	Roof Frame Material	Assessor's Classification	UPD-ICE Structural System	Beam Material and Bracing System
		1 - Reinforced Concrete			1 - Reinforced Concrete
1 - Good	1 - None	2 - Steel	1 - I-A	1 - W1 or W2	2 - Steel
2 - Fair	2 - 0-0.5 meters 3 - 1.0-2.5 meters	3 - Wood	2 - I-B	2 - W3	3 - Wood
3 - Poor	4 - 2.5-5.0 meters		3 - I-C	3 - N	4 - Unknown
4 - Under Construction	5 - >5 meters	4 - Unknown 5 - none	4 - II-A 5 - II-B	4 - CWS 5 - CHB	5 - None

| | | 6 - II-C | 6 - URM | |
| | | 7 - II-D | 7 - URA | |

Seismic
Separation
(Right)

		8 - III-A	8 - RM1	Column Material
				1 - Reinforced
1 - None		9 - III-B	9 - RM2	Concrete
	Floor Frame			
2 - 0-0.5 meters	Material	10 - III-C	10 - C1	2 – Steel
3 - 1.0-2.5	1 - Reinforced			
meters	Concrete	11- III-D	11 - C2	3 – Wood
4 - 2.5-5.0				
meters	2 – Steel	12 - III-E	12 - C4	4 – Unknown
5 - >5 meters	3 – Wood	13 - IV	13 - PC1	5 - None
	4 – Unknown	14 - Other	14 - PC2	
		15 -		
	5 - none	Unknown	15 - S1	
			16 - S2	
			17 - S3	
			18 - S4	
			19 -	
			Unknown	

6. Building Database

Roofing Material Support	Roof System	Internal Wall Materials	Opening in Walls	Num Basement Levels
A1 - Wooden Purlins	1 - Unknown	1 - Unknown	1 - 5 to 10 sqm	1 - 1 level
2 - Steel Purlins	2 - Gable	2 - Particle Board	2 - 10 to 15 sqm	2 - 2 levels
3 - Unknown	3 - Hip	3 - Gypsum Board	3 - 15 to 20 sqm	3 - 3 levels
	4 - Dome	4 - Hardiflex	4 - 20 to 25 sqm	4 - 4 levels
Roofing Material Fastening	5 - Flat	5 - Plywood	5 - 25 to 30 sqm	5 - 5 levels
1 - Unknown	6 - Attic Type	6 - Lawanit	6 - 30 to 40 sqm	6 - > 6 levels
2 - Nails	7 - Complex	7 - Plaster Board	7 - 40 to 50 sqm	7 - none
3 - Wire		8 - Cement Board	8 - 50 to 60 sqm	
	Roof Frame System			Above Ground Car Parking:
4 - Screws			9 - 60 to 70 sqm	
5 - Glued	1 - Wood	Floor Materials	10 - 70 to 80 sqm	1 Yes
	2 - Steel	1 - Wood	11 - 80 to 90 sqm	2 No
Roof Frame to Column Connection	3 - Concrete	2 - Ceramic Tiles	12 - 90 to 100 sqm	
1 - Unknown	4 - Unknown	3 - Vinyl tiles	13 - >100 sqm	
2 - Hooked	5 - None	4 - Linoleum		
3 - Riveted		5 – Carpet		
4 - Bolted		6 - None		
5 - Welded				

7. ROOF WALLS

Roof 1 Type/Roof 2 Type	Roof 1 Percent	Roof Attachment Height	Other Roof Attachment
1 - Galvanized Iron/Aluminum	by 10% intrval	1 - none	1 - TV Antenna
2 - Aluminum		2 - 0 to 1 meters	2 - Transmission Tower
3 - Tile Concrete	Main Roof Attachment	3 - 1 to 2 meters	3 - Air conditioning

		4 - 2 to 4 meters	4 - Exhaust or Ventilation outlet
4 - Clay	1 - Billboard	5 - 4 to 6 meters	5 - Solar panels
5 - Wood	2 - TV antenna	6 - 6 to 8 meters	6 - Parapet
6 - Cogon	3 - Transmission tower	7 - 8 to 10 meters	7 - Steeple
7 - Nipa	4 - Air conditioning		
	5 - Exhaust or tv ventilation outlet	8 > 10 meters	8 - Other
8 - Anahaw			
9 - Asbestos	6 - Solar panels		
10 - Mixed Galvanized Iron & Concrete		Roof Pitch	
11 - Synthetic tile	7 - Parapet	1 - Gentle	5 – Dome
12 - Unknown	8 - Steeple	2 - Moderate	6 - Mixed
		3 - Steep	7 - Other
		4 - Curved	8 – Unknown

Roof
Decoration:_____

8. FAÇADE AND FLOOR

Floor System	Floor Elevation from Street	Sub-floor footprint	Sub-floor use	Foundation
1 - On-ground	1 - > 2 meters	1 - Unknown	1 - noner	1 - Hard rock
2 - Partially elevated	2 - 1.5 to 2.0 meters	2 - 0%	2 - Dwelling	2 - Rock
3 - Wholly elevated	3 - 0.5 to 1.0 meters	3 - 10%	3 - Workshop	3 - Dense soil and soft rock
4 - Unknown	4 - 0.25 to 0.5 meters	4 - 20%	4 - Bathroom	4 - Stiff soil profile
	5 - 0 meters	5 - 30%	5 - Laundry	5 - Soft soil
Floor Type	6 - 0 to -.25 meters	6 - 40%	7 - Storage	6 - Unknown
1 - None	7 - -0.5 to -2.0 meters	7 - 50%	8 - Other	
2 - Wood	8 - -1.0 to -1.5 meters	8 - 60%	9 - Unknown	Maximum Floor Level
3 - Concrete	9 - -1.5 to -2 meters	9 - 70%		1 - 1 to 2 meters
			Basement Present?	
4 - Bamboo	10 - >-2.0 meters	10 - 80%	1 - Yes	2 - 2 to 3 meters
5 - Stone		11 - 90%	2 - No	3 - 3 to 4 meters
6 - Steel	Ground Slope	12 - 100%		4 - 4 to 5 meters
7 - Unknown	1 - Flat (0% to 15%)			5 - 5 to 6 meters
	2 - Gentle (5% to 15%)			6 - 6 to 7 meters
	3 - Moderate (15% to 25%)			7 - 7 to 8 meters
	4 - Steep (>25%)			8 - 8 t0 9 meters
				9 - 9 to 10 meters

Appendix 2a:

Approved letter request to conduct survey in the City of Tuguegarao

Republic of the Philippines
CAGAYAN STATE UNIVERSITY
Carig, Tuguegarao City
Office of the Director of Research in Engineering, IT, and Natural Sciences

April 18, 2013

Hon. DELFIN T. TING
City Mayor
Tuguegarao City

The Regional Disaster Science and Management S&T Capacity Development for SUCs with nodal center at the Cagayan State University-Carig campus have chosen the City of Tuguegarao as a pilot area in the implementation of a research-based capacity building activity utilizing state-of-the-art technology developed by Philippine Institute of Volcanology and Seismology (PHIVOLCS). This activity called Capacity Enhancement of Academic Researchers on Hazard, Risk and Exposure Database Development through the use of the Rapid Earthquake Damage Assessment Software (REDAS) involves data gathering on critical structures in the locality to include residential, commercial/industrial buildings, key government structures like offices, schools, evacuation centers and the like. Any information generated from this activity will help in the rapid assessment of a calamity as implied in the software.

On April 24-30, 2013, a team from CSU-Carig will conduct a survey of barangay Carig being the regional center and in the city proper where majority of transactions transpire 24/7.

In this regard, may we seek permission from your good office to allow our team to conduct said activity. Rest assured that we will furnish your office of whatever output we shall come up with this endeavor.

Attached herewith is the sample survey form for your perusal.

Sincerely,

Engr. POLICARPIO L. MABBORANG, JR.
Study Leader- CSU

APPROVED

Noted:

DELFIN TELAN TING
City Mayor

Engr. ARTHUR G. IBANEZ, Ph. D.
Campus Executive Officer- Carig Campus

Appendix 2b:

Approved letter request to conduct survey in the City of Tuguegarao

Republic of the Philippines
CAGAYAN STATE UNIVERSITY
Carig, Tuguegarao City

July 16, 2013

Hon. JEFFERSON P. SORIANO
City Mayor
Tuguegarao City

The Regional Disaster Science and Management S&T Capacity Development Project for SUCs with nodal center at the Cagayan State University-Carig campus have chosen the City of Tuguegarao as a pilot area in the implementation of a research-based capacity building activity utilizing state-of-the-art technology developed by the Philippine Institute of Volcanology and Seismology (PHIVOLCS). This activity called Capacity Enhancement of Academic Researchers on Hazard, Risk and Exposure Database.Development through the use of the Rapid Earthquake Damage Assessment Software (REDAS) involves data gathering on building structures in the locality to include residential, commercial/industrial buildings, key government structures like offices, schools, evacuation centers and the like. Any information generated from this activity will help in the rapid assessment of a calamity as implied in the software.

The project started gathering data in May of this year, yet, we need to collect more to suffice the activity requirements. As a matter of procedure, the survey team coordinates will the barangay officials for general information and possible assistance from them.

In this regard, may we seek permission from your good office to allow our team to conduct said activity. Rest assured that we will furnish your office of whatever output we shall come up with this endeavor.

Attached herewith is the sample survey form for your perusal.

Sincerely,

Engr. POLICARPIO L. MABBORANG, JR.
Study Leader- CSU

ATTY. RONALD L. BRILLANTES
City Administrator

Noted:

Engr. ARTHUR G. IBANEZ, Ph. D.
Campus Executive Officer- Carig Campus

55

Appendix 3:

Table A1. PHIVOLCS Earthquake Intensity Scale (PEIS)

Intensity Scale	Description
I	**Scarcely Perceptible** Perceptible to people under favorable circumstances. Delicately balanced objects are disturbed slightly. Still water in containers oscillates slowly.
II	**Slightly Felt** Felt by few individuals at rest indoors. Hanging objects swings lightly. Still Water in containers oscillates noticeably.
III	**Weak** Felt by many people indoors especially in upper floors of buildings. Vibration is felt like one passing of a light truck. Dizziness and nausea are experienced by some people. Hanging objects swing moderately. Still water in containers oscillates moderately.
IV	**Moderately Strong** Felt generally by people indoors and by some people outdoors. Light sleepers are awakened. Vibration is felt like a passing of heavy truck. Hanging objects swing considerably. Dinner, plates, glasses, windows and doors rattle. Floors and walls of wood framed buildings creak. Standing motor cars may rock slightly. Liquids in containers are slightly disturbed. Water in containers oscillate strongly. Rumbling sound may sometimes be heard.
V	**Strong** Generally felt by most people indoors and outdoors. Many sleeping people are awakened. Some are frightened, some run outdoors. Strong shaking and rocking felt throughout building. Hanging objects swing violently. Dining utensils clatter and clink; some are broken. Small, light and unstable objects may fall or overturn. Liquids spill from filled open containers. Standing vehicles rock noticeably. Shaking of leaves and twigs of trees are noticeable.
VI	**Very Strong** Many people are frightened; many run outdoors. Some people lose their balance. Motorists feel like driving in flat tires. Heavy objects or furniture move or may be shifted. Small church bells may ring. Wall plaster may crack. Very old or poorly built houses and man-made structures are slightly damaged though well-built structures are not affected. Limited rockfalls and rolling boulders occur in hilly to mountainous areas and escarpments. Trees are noticeably shaken.
VII	**Destructive** Most people are frightened and run outdoors. People find it difficult to stand in upper floors. Heavy objects and furniture overturn or topple. Big church bells may ring. Old or poorly-built structures suffer considerable damage. Some well-built structures are slightly damaged. Some cracks may appear on dikes, fish ponds, road surface, or concrete hollow block walls. Limited liquefaction, lateral spreading and landslides are observed. Trees are shaken strongly. (Liquefaction is a process by which

		loose saturated sand lose strength during an earthquake and behave like liquid).
	VIII	**Very Destructive** People panicky. People find it difficult to stand even outdoors. Many well-built buildings are considerably damaged. Concrete dikes and foundation of bridges are destroyed by ground settling or toppling. Railway tracks are bent or broken. Tombstones may be displaced, twisted or overturned. Utility posts, towers and monuments mat tilt or topple. Water and sewer pipes may be bent, twisted or broken. Liquefaction and lateral spreading cause man- made structure to sink, tilt or topple. Numerous landslides and rockfalls occur in mountainous and hilly areas. Boulders are thrown out from their positions particularly near the epicenter. Fissures and faults rapture maybe observed. Trees are violently shaken. Water splash or stop over dikes or banks of rivers.
	IX	**Devastating** People are forcibly thrown to ground. Many cry and shake with fear. Most buildings are totally damaged. Bridges and elevated concrete structures are toppled or destroyed. Numerous utility posts, towers and monument are tilted, toppled or broken. Water sewer pipes are bent, twisted or broken. Landslides and liquefaction with lateral spreadings and sandboils are widespread. The ground is distorted into undulations. Trees are shaken very violently with some toppled or broken. Boulders are commonly thrown out. River water splashes violently on slops over dikes and banks.
	X	**Completely Devastating** Practically all man-made structures are destroyed. Massive landslides and liquefaction, large scale subsidence and uplifting of land forms and many ground fissures are observed. Changes in river courses and destructive seiches in large lakes occur. Many trees are toppled, broken and uprooted.

Appendix 3.

Landuse Plan of Tuguegarao City for 2013-2022

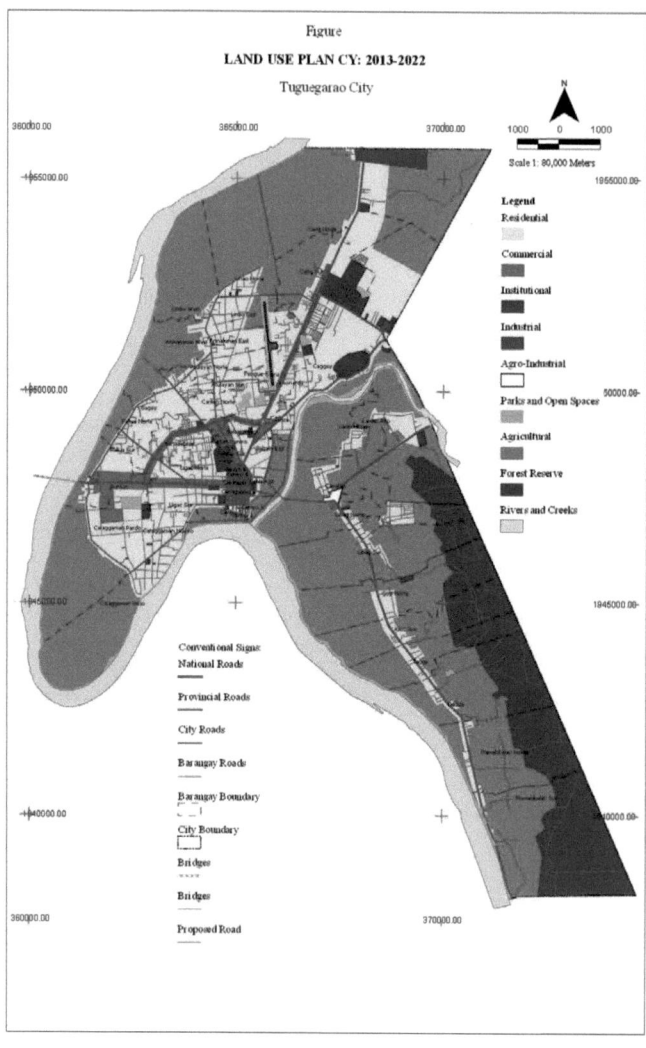

Appendix 4.

Table A2. Summary of building categories according to use.

Bldg use	Carig Sur	Centro 6	Centro 10	Total
Residential	725	30	364	1119
Commercial	15			15
Industrial	4	11		15
Hospital	1	1		2
Government	75	4	1	80
Office	9	3	3	15
Agriculture	1	1		2
Bank		1		1
Others	32	37	17	86
Total	862	88	385	1335

Appendix 5.

Sample building photographs taken from Carig Sur.

Cagayan State University – Carig Campus   Botica Paraggua along Maharlika Hiway

Department of Environment & Natural Resources – Region 2

Cagayan Valley Medical Center

Appendix 6.

Sample building photographs taken from Centro 6.

Fastfoods along Bonifacio St.

Hotel along Luna St.

Paseo Reale Mall

Tuguegarao People's General Hospital

Appendix 7.

Sample building photographs taken from Centro 10.

Provincial Jail

Mosque

Hotel Lorita

Sts. Peter & Paul Cathedral

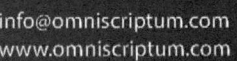

Printed by Books on Demand GmbH, Norderstedt / Germany